FREE
INDEED

A GUIDE TO COOKING GLUTEN-FREE, DAIRY-FREE, SOY-FREE AND FREE OF ALL PROCESSED SUGARS

LEAH G. KNIGHT

authorHOUSE®

AuthorHouse™
1663 Liberty Drive
Bloomington, IN 47403
www.authorhouse.com
Phone: 1-800-839-8640

Published by AuthorHouse   01/22/2015

ISBN: 978-1-4969-4491-7 (sc)
ISBN: 978-1-4969-4493-1 (hc)
ISBN: 978-1-4969-4492-4 (e)

Library of Congress Control Number: 2014918077

FRONT COVER RECIPES

Strawberry Lemonade
Fresh Herb Salad with Basil Salad Dressing
Garlic Spaghetti Squash
Delicious Dinner Rolls
Desert Cactus Meatballs
Dark Chocolate Peanut Butter Cups

BACK COVER RECIPE

Cinnamon Rolls

DEDICATION

To my husband Jason, who always encourages me to try new things, and who eats whatever I create without complaint.

To my mother Brenda, who has taught me the joy and fulfillment of cooking.

To my father Dan, who has worked hard to make it possible for Mom to be a stay-at-home mother and teacher.

To those who are searching for practical and delicious recipes while following a focused dietary plan.

AUTHOR'S ACKNOWLEDGEMENTS

I would like to thank my close and extended family for their constant support during the creation of this book; my brother Seth for his dedication to health and fitness; Darrik and Stacie Walker for their friendship and for their creative influence; and to Jim Clapper, owner of DIY Wood Studio, for his time and for his generous donation of the wooden artifacts used in this book's photography.

A special thank you to Madison Bartz of "That's Nice" Photography for her creative photographs; to my brother Joel for his spontaneous assistance designing additional pictures; and to Eddie and Annie Ferguson for generously allowing the photographs to be taken on their beautiful property.

A very special thank you to Dr. Todd Ferguson N.D. for his dietary instruction and for his endorsement; and to Dr. Christopher Danduran D.C., D.A.C.N.B., F.A.C.F.N., for his enthusiastic support and for his endorsement.

DISCLAIMER

The recipes, directions and information found in this book are intended to provide healthy choices for those with dietary restrictions. This book is not intended to diagnose or cure any particular disease or disorder. Diagnosis of any condition should only be made by a qualified physician. Neither the author nor the publisher is liable for any negative outcome resulting from the information, preparation or application of dietary suggestions contained in this book. The product reference list and websites listed are provided as informational resources only and do not constitute product endorsement. The websites or products listed in this book may change.

Children under the age of one should avoid raw honey, cow's milk and peanut butter. Avoid feeding infants food that is too soft and sticky, small and hard, or too large. Introduce new foods only under a qualified doctor's supervision.

Neither the author nor the publisher is responsible for the allergic needs of the reader. Introduce possible allergens such as nuts or molasses only under a qualified doctor's supervision.

ENDORSEMENT

Dr. Todd Ferguson, N.D.
Prairie Naturopathic Doctors

"As a Naturopathic Doctor I encounter on a daily basis the havoc excessive sugar intake and food sensitivities can cause and the amazing return to health good nutrition can bring about. The steady increase in processed sugar in the standard diet has led to a steady decline in human health. Greater than two-thirds of Americans are overweight and what used to be "adult" disorders, namely obesity and type-two diabetes, are now commonly seen in children. Increased processed sugar in the diet worsens digestion contributing to increased reactivity to foods and a decline in nutritional status. Sensitivities to gluten and dairy are two of the most common reactions I see in my practice with far reaching effects. Food sensitivities go beyond digestive disturbances as I commonly see dairy and gluten removal from the diet improve headaches, fatigue, insomnia, joint pain, autoimmune conditions and more. I have also seen people on a "health kick" who start consuming an abundance of soy products react to this change poorly. Thyroid conditions can start or worsen by greatly increasing soy consumption. Suffice it to say everyone can benefit by decreasing the amount of processed sugar in their diet and many may benefit from removing common sensitivities. As the commercial food industry making foods laden with processed sugar, dairy, and gluten has overtaken the kitchen and the grocery store it has become all the more important to have a resource for making nutritious foods free off processed sugar. Thank you, Leah Knight for making this wonderful resource of tasty whole foods."

Dr. Todd Ferguson, Prairie Naturopathic Doctors

ENDORSEMENT

Dr. Christopher Danduran, D.C., D.A.C.N.B., F.A.C.F.N.
ACA Board Certified Chiropractic Neurologist
Diplomat of the American Chiropractic Neurology Board
Fellow of the American College of Functional Neurology
Clinical Director of Dakota Health Solutions

"The food choices and concepts laid out in this book have been pivotal in my practice not only for patients with metabolic struggles but also resistant neurological conditions. Clinical studies have illustrated the benefit of a hypoallergenic and anti-inflammatory regimen on chronic diseases of all kinds that plague industrialized countries today. As a clinic serving patients nationwide, this dietary foundation has been instrumental in a multitude of the cases for its ability to set up the metabolic capacity and the neurological potential essential for healing. Free Indeed is a must read for those who struggle with chronic metabolic, inflammatory, and neurologic ailments and who are truly committed to incorporating the health benefits of a gluten-free, dairy-free, soy-free and processed sugar-free diet."

Dr. Christopher Danduran, Dakota Health Solutions

TABLE OF CONTENTS

INTRODUCTION/COOK BOOK BASICS

The goal of this book is to provide delicious recipes for those who are seeking variety while maintaining a restricted diet. The primary focus of this book is for instruction in the creation of a perfect and fluffy loaf of gluten-free bread, or a batch of gluten-free biscuits, or a pan of gluten-free muffins, while using organic dairy, soy and unrefined sugar substitutes.

When cooking gluten-free, it is extremely important to find an effective flour blend. This book offers a variety of gluten-free flour blends, providing a suitable flour option for any dietary need. Each blend is equally successful and produces identical results when used according to the specific mixing directions found in this book.

It is always best to choose organic ingredients whenever possible.

Refer to the product reference list for assistance with purchasing ingredients and product availability.

PASTRY BAKING TIPS

It is extremely important to mix ingredients in the proper order when cooking gluten, dairy, soy, and sugar-free. If the ingredients are combined according to typical flour instructions (for pastry containing gluten,) the outcome will be breads, biscuits and muffins that do not rise, are extremely dense, and are often very dry and crumbly. However, if all substituted ingredients are mixed in the proper manner, at the right moment, the outcome can be FANTASTIC!

How to bake a FLUFFY loaf of gluten, dairy, soy and sugar-free pastry such as bread:

The art of baking gluten-free is an exact science. All the measurements should be as precise as possible to ensure a good result.

Do not double a bread or pastry recipe to get more than one loaf. Instead, simply make two separate loaves. Doubling or halving a recipe can cause the mixture to be incorrect.

FLOUR PREPARATION

1. Choose the gluten-free flour blend variation that suits your dietary restrictions, and purchase all the necessary organic ingredients.

2. Carefully follow the blend directions to create the perfect flour.

3. Store the blend in the refrigerator or freezer in a sealed container to maintain the flour's freshness.

BAKING PREPARATION AND INSTRUCTIONS

1. In the bowl of a stand mixer, combine ONLY the dry ingredients (flour, salt, yeast, etc.) and mix for 2 minutes using the whisk attachment.
2. While continuing to mix, slowly add in the warm water or milk.
3. If the recipe contains honey and butter, melt the two together and cool until lukewarm before adding.
4. At this point, add any extra ingredients such as mashed bananas or other fruit.
5. If using eggs, add them in now.
6. Beat the entire mixture on high for 3 minutes.
7. Using a rubber spatula, gently stir down the sides of the batter and beat on high for another 2 minutes to add air to the dough.
8. If the bread contains yeast, cover the mixing bowl and allow the dough to rise for 1–2 hours or until it doubles in size.
9. When the dough has risen, carefully scoop the batter into a prepared pan.
10. Add one spoonful of water to the top of the dough. Using a wet spatula, GENTLY smooth out the dough to meet the edges of the pan.

11. THE MOST IMPORTANT KEY TO GLUTEN-FREE BAKING IS A LIGHT TOUCH!
12. If the recipe contains yeast, cover the pan with a piece of buttered parchment paper, allow the dough to rise for another hour or until it has risen above the edges of the pan.
13. Preheat the oven to the desired temperature while the bread is rising.
14. When the bread has adequately risen, remove the parchment paper and bake for the prescribed time. (It is important not to overcook gluten-free bread.)
15. When the bread is done, remove it from the pan and cool for at least 15 minutes before serving.
16. Gluten-free bread or pastry is best when it is still warm from the oven. The shelf life of gluten-free bread is shorter than that of wheat bread. Therefore, it is important to place the bread in a sealed container or bag and store it in the refrigerator to preserve its freshness.

PRODUCT REF

1. Applegate Natural Turke͟ (sugar)
2. Arrowhead Mills Creamy ͟er
3. Arrowhead Mills Organic Buc
4. Arrowhead Mills Organic Yellow͟ Meal
5. Barbara's Organic Brown Rice Crisͅ ͟s
6. Bob's Red Mill All Natural Cornstarch
7. Bob's Red Mill Baking Powder (aluminum-free)
8. Bob's Red Mill Baking Soda
9. Bob's Red Mill Organic Brown Rice
10. Bob's Red Mill Organic Whole Ground Flax Meal
11. Bob's Red Mill Potato Starch
12. Bob's Red Mill Shredded Coconut
13. Bob's Red Mill Tapioca Starch
14. Bob's Red Mill Xanthan Gum
15. Braga Organic Farms Assorted Nuts
16. Bubbies Pickles
17. Bubbies Sauer Kraut
18. By Bee Foods Organic Frozen Vegetables
19. Coleman Organic Chicken Breast, Whole Chicken
20. Costal Range Organic Ground Turkey
21. DeBole Gluten Free Rice Pasta
22. Earth Balance Butter (dairy-free and soy-free)
23. Earth Balance Mayonnaise
24. Eden Foods 100% Soba Buckwheat Noodles
25. Eden Foods Organic Beans
26. Eden Foods, Organic Brown Rice Vinegar
27. Eden Organic Sesame Oil
28. Farmer's Market Organic Pumpkin
29. Full Circle Organic Balsamic Vinegar
30. Full Circle Organic Pasta Sauce
31. Full Circle Organic Spaghetti Sauce
32. Full Circle Refried Beans
33. Full Circle Yellow Mustard
34. Glory Bee Organic Clover Honey
35. Go Veggie Dairy-Free Cheese

36. Hain's Organic Beef Broth
37. Hain's Pure Sea Salt
38. Healthworks Raw Certified Organic Cocoa Powder
39. Italian Volcano Organic Lemon Juice
40. Kirkland Signature Organic Chicken Stock
41. Kirkland Signature Organic Eggs
42. Kirkland Signature Organic Extra Virgin Olive Oil
43. Kirkland Signature Organic Ground Beef
44. Kirkland Signature Organic Potato Chips (sea salt)
45. Kirkland Signature Organic Tortilla Chips (sea salt)
46. Kirkland Signature Organic Coconut Oil
47. Kirkland Signature Organic Diced Tomatoes
48. Kirkland Signature Organic Tomato Paste
49. Kirkland Signature Organic Tomato Sauce
50. La Preferida Organic Green Chilies
51. McCormick Organic Spices
52. Mediterranean Organic Ripe Pitted Black Olives
53. Mother Earth Organic Mushrooms
54. Native Forest Unsweetened Coconut Milk
55. Natural Delights Medjool Dates
56. Natural Planet Purple Potato Chips (sea salt)
57. NOW Foods, Real Food Raw Pumpkin Seeds
58. Nutiva Organic Chia Seeds
59. Plantation Unsulphered Black Strap Molasses
60. Rapunzel Organic Active Dry Yeast
61. Rapunzel Organic Corn Starch
62. Rice Dream Organic Rice Milk
63. Simply Organic Spices
64. Simply Organic Vanilla Extract (sugar-free)
65. So Delicious Unsweetened Coconut Yogurt
66. Spectrum Naturals Organic Distilled White Vinegar
67. Spectrum Organic Non-hydrogenated Vegetable Shortening
68. Sun Organic Farm Assorted Nuts
69. Thai Kitchen Organic Full Fat Unsweetened Coconut Milk
70. Wholesome Sweeteners Organic Agave Nectar
71. Woodstock Farms – All Natural Raw Almond Butter
72. Wyman's Frozen Fruits and Berries

*These items can be purchased at a health food store or one of the following websites:

Amazon.com
Costco.com
Azurestandard.com
Mountainroseherbs.com

KNIGHT'S NUTRITIOUS GLUTEN-FREE FLOUR BLEND

VARIATION 1:
Preparation time: 10 minutes
Yields: 12 cups

Ingredients:
7 cups organic brown rice flour
1 cup organic corn starch
2 cups organic tapioca flour
¾ cup organic potato starch
2 Tbsp. organic xanthan gum
2 Tbsp. organic flax meal (optional)

VARIATION 2:
Preparation time: 10 minutes
Yields: 11 cups

Ingredients:
7 cups organic brown rice flour
2 cups organic corn starch
2 cups organic tapioca flour
2 Tbsp. organic xanthan gum
2 Tbsp. organic flax meal (optional)

VARIATION 3:
Preparation time: 10 minutes
Yields: 11 ½ cups

Ingredients:
7 cups organic brown rice flour
2 cups organic tapioca flour
2 cups organic potato starch
2 Tbsp. organic xanthan gum
2 Tbsp. organic flax meal (optional)

Instructions:
In the bowl of a stand mixer, combine all the ingredients and mix for 2 minutes. Using a spatula, stir the flour blend being sure to bring the flour from the bottom of the bowl to the top. Mix again for 2 minutes. Pour into a container, seal, and store in the refrigerator or freezer between uses.

FLOUR BLENDS

APPETIZERS, SNACKS & BEVERAGES

STRAWBERRY LEMONADE

APPETIZERS, SNACKS & BEVERAGES

BANANA FLAX OATMEAL

Preparation time: 10 minutes
Cook time: 3 minutes
Yields: 1½ cups

Ingredients:
1 cup organic coconut milk, unsweetened
½ cup organic GF oats
1 Tbsp. organic flax meal
½ organic banana, sliced
2 Tbsp. organic walnuts, chopped (optional)

Instructions:
Pour the coconut milk into a small pan and bring it to a boil. Add in the oats and flax meal. Stir thoroughly. Remove it from heat and cover it for 5 minutes or until the oats are soft. Cool and add in the banana slices and walnuts. Serve and enjoy!

CHIA FRUIT BITES

Preparation time: 10 minutes
Cook time: 13 minutes
Yields: 16

Ingredients:
¾ cup Knight's Nutritious GF Flour Blend
2 Tbsp. organic chia seeds
1 tsp. organic nutmeg
1 tsp. organic cinnamon
¼ tsp. organic sea salt
½ tsp. organic baking soda
1 cage-free organic egg
1 ripe organic banana, mashed*
1 Tbsp. organic coconut oil, melted
⅛ cup organic coconut milk, unsweetened
1 tsp. pure organic vanilla extract
¼ cup organic walnuts (optional)

Instructions:
Preheat oven to 350 degrees.
In the bowl of a stand mixer, combine the flour, seeds, nutmeg, cinnamon, salt, and soda. Mix until well combined. In a separate bowl, mash the banana* and mix with the egg and oil and set aside. While mixing, add in the milk to the dry ingredients until a crumbly texture is achieved. Finally, add the remaining wet ingredients to the dry ingredients. Beat it on high for 2-3 minutes to add air to the batter. Spoon the batter into the cups of a well-buttered mini muffin pan. Cook for 13 minutes or until the tops of the muffins are golden brown. Cool and serve.

*Variation 1: Add in ½ cup of chopped fresh raspberries or fresh strawberries in place of the banana.

CHICKEN AVOCADO WRAP

Preparation time: 5 minutes
Cook time: 0 minutes
Serves: 2

Ingredients:
1 Tbsp. organic mayonnaise
1 Tbsp. organic yellow mustard
4 slices free-range organic chicken breast, cooked
2 slices fresh organic tomato
¼ fresh organic avocado, sliced
1 recipe Tender Tortillas*
1 fresh organic onion, sliced (optional)
Organic lettuce (optional)

Instructions:
Make one recipe of Tender Tortillas and use two tortillas (refrigerate or freeze the extra tortillas.) Spread the mayo and mustard completely over one side of each tortilla. In the center of the tortilla, layer the turkey, tomato, avocado, and additional vegetables if desired. Roll or fold it into a wrap and enjoy!

*See recipe for Tender Tortillas

DEVILED EGGS

Preparation time: 10 minutes
Cook time: 0 minutes.
Yields: 12

Ingredients:
6 cage-free organic eggs
2 Tbsp. organic mayonnaise
2 tsp. organic yellow mustard
1 Tbsp. organic pickle juice
Dash of organic sea salt, to taste
Dash of organic black pepper, to taste
Dash of organic paprika, garnish

Instructions:
In a medium sized sauce pan, hard-boil the eggs. Cool and peel. Slice into halves and remove yolk. Place yolks in a small bowl and mash. Add in remaining ingredients and mix well. Scoop or pipe yolk filling into hollow of each egg white. Garnish with a dash of paprika and serve.

GLAZED NUTS

Preparation time: 10 minutes
Cook time: 5-7 minutes
Yields: 2 cups

Ingredients:
2 cups organic walnuts (or any nut of your choice)
⅓ cup pure organic maple syrup
⅛ tsp. pure organic vanilla extract
Dash of organic sea salt

Instructions:
Combine syrup, vanilla, and salt in a skillet. Warm over medium heat. Add walnuts (or nut of your choice) stirring continually until syrup begins to caramelize. Remove from heat, stirring continually for 1 minute. Place walnuts on a piece of wax paper or buttered parchment paper until cool.

*Variation: For Cinnamon Glazed Nuts: Add 1-2 Tbsp. of organic cinnamon to taste.

GUACAMOLE

Preparation time: 15 minutes
Chill time: 30 minutes
Yields: 2-3 cups

Ingredients:
2 large ripe organic avocados, cubed
2-3 Tbsp. organic lemon juice
½ tsp. organic garlic powder
1 Tbsp. fresh organic cilantro, chopped
2-4 organic green chilies, chopped
1 medium organic tomato, peeled, seeded, and chopped
1 organic jalapeno or serrano pepper, chopped (optional)
Pinch of organic sea salt, to taste

Instructions:
In a small bowl, combine all ingredients and chill for 30 minutes. Serve with organic corn or rice chips.

NO BAKE CEREAL BARS

Preparation time: 15 minutes
Chill time: 1 hour
Yields: 16 bars

Ingredients:
½ cup organic creamy peanut butter (sugar-free)
⅓ cup organic clover honey
⅓ cup assorted nuts (optional)
⅛ cup unsulphured black strap molasses
¼ cup pure organic maple syrup
1 cup organic GF oats
1 cup GF organic brown rice crispies

Instructions:
Line an 8x8 pan with wax or parchment paper and set aside.

Combine peanut butter, honey, molasses, and syrup in a small sauce pan and warm until very creamy. Do not overcook it! In a separate bowl, combine rice crispies and sauce by gently pouring peanut butter mixture over rice crispies. Mix until all cereal has been coated with peanut butter, taking care not to crush cereal. Next, add oats and assorted nuts. Mix thoroughly. Pour into prepared pan and press the mixture evenly to all sides with well-buttered fingers. Chill, cut, and enjoy!

BLUEBERRY-COCONUT-CHIA SMOOTHIE

Preparation time: 10 minutes
Chill time: 0 minutes
Yields: 1 smoothie

Ingredients:
½ cup frozen organic blueberries
½ cup fresh organic spinach
½ cup organic plain coconut yogurt, unsweetened
½ cup frozen organic strawberries
1 Tbsp. organic chia seeds

Instructions:
Combine ingredients in a food processor and blend on high until smooth. Serve immediately in a chilled glass.

CREAMY PEANUT BUTTER SMOOTHIE

Preparation time: 10 minutes
Chill time: 0 minutes
Yields: 1 smoothie

Ingredients:
1 organic ripe banana
1 organic apple, sliced
1-2 Tbsp. organic agave nectar, to taste
2 Tbsp. organic smooth peanut butter
1 cup crushed ice
1 tsp. pure organic vanilla extract

Instructions:
Combine ingredients in a food processor and blend on high until creamy. Serve immediately in a chilled glass.

CREAMY PEANUT BUTTER SMOOTHIE

LEMON-STRAWBERRY-CUCUMBER ICE WATER

Preparation time: 5 minutes
Chill time: 12 hours
Yields: 1 gallon

Ingredients:
2 cups fresh organic cucumbers, sliced
2 cups fresh organic strawberries, washed and stemmed
2 fresh organic lemons, thinly sliced
¼ cup organic agave nectar
4 cups ice cubes
Ice water

Instructions:
In a large bowl, combine fruit slices. Coat with agave nectar. This will bring out the natural fruit flavors. Next, in a gallon glass jar, layer the ice and fruit until all the ice and fruit is used. Finally, fill the remaining space in the jar with ice water. Seal the jar securely and refrigerate for 12 hours until strongly fruit-flavored.

LEMON-STRAWBERRY-KALE SMOOTHIE

Preparation time: 10 minutes
Chill time: 0 minutes
Yields: 1 smoothie

Ingredients:
1 cup fresh organic kale, washed
1 cup frozen organic strawberries
⅛ cup fresh organic lemon juice
⅛ cup organic agave nectar
½ cup crushed ice
½ cup ice water

Instructions:
Combine the ingredients in a food processor and blend on high until smooth. Serve immediately in a chilled glass.

STRAWBERRY- BLUEBERRY- BANANA SMOOTHIE

Preparation time: 5 minutes
Chill time: 0 minutes
Serves: 1 smoothie

Ingredients:
1 large organic banana, halved
5 large frozen organic strawberries
½ cup frozen organic blueberries
⅛ cup organic agave nectar
Dash of organic lemon juice, chilled

Instructions:
Using a food processor, thoroughly blend all ingredients together. Serve immediately in a chilled glass.

STRAWBERRY LEMONADE

Preparation time: 10 minutes
Chill time: 1-2 hours
Serves: 1 gallon

Ingredients:
1¼ cup fresh organic lemon juice
2 pints fresh or frozen organic strawberries
½ cup organic agave nectar
2 quarts ice water

Instructions:
If using fresh strawberries, remove stems and wash. In a food processor, blend strawberries and agave nectar. Combine all ingredients in a gallon glass pitcher and mix thoroughly. For best flavor, chill for at least 2 hours. Serve with a slice of fresh lemon.

SOUPS, SALADS & VEGETABLES

ASSORTED SALADS AND VEGETABLES

SOUPS, SALADS & VEGETABLES

CACCIATORE SOUP

Preparation time: 10 minutes
Cook time: 3-4 hours
Serves: 5

Ingredients:
¼ cup organic capers, drained
3 cups chicken, cooked and cubed
1 tsp. organic sea salt
¼ tsp. organic black pepper
2 tsp. organic oregano
½ tsp. organic red pepper flakes
1 Tbsp. extra virgin olive oil
1 organic red pepper, chopped
1 organic green pepper, chopped
1 small organic onion, chopped
2 Tbsp. organic minced garlic
2 (15 oz.) cans organic diced tomatoes
1 cup organic chicken broth
1 tsp. organic parsley
1 tsp. organic basil
½ cup dry organic brown rice

Instructions:
In a large crock pot, combine all ingredients and cook on high for 3-4 hours. Serve with Fantastically Fluffy French Bread.*

*See recipe for Fantastically Fluffy French Bread

CHICKEN SOUP

Preparation time: 15 minutes
Cook time: 15 minutes
Serves: 4

Ingredients:
1 quart organic chicken stock
1 rib organic celery, diced
1 large organic carrot, diced
1-2 Tbsp. extra virgin olive oil
½ cup organic onion, chopped
1½ tsp organic thyme
1 organic bay leaf
1 tsp. organic minced garlic
1-1 ½ cup free-range organic chicken, cooked and cubed
Dash of organic sea salt, to taste
Dash of organic black pepper, to taste
1 small organic zucchini or spaghetti squash, made into noodles (follow the preparation instructions for Garlic Spaghetti Squash. * Leave out the spices)

Instructions:
Coat the bottom of a large sauce pan with oil. Add in the celery, carrots, garlic, thyme, and bay leaf and sauté until tender. Add stock to the sautéed vegetables and bring to a rapid boil. Reduce heat and simmer. Add squash and continue to heat for 5-10 minutes. Add in the chicken and mix well. Season with salt and pepper. Serve with buttered Bodacious Brown Bread.*

*See recipe for Bodacious Brown Bread
*See recipe for Garlic Spaghetti Squash (noodles)

CREAM SOUP

Preparation time: 5 minutes
Cook time: 20 minutes
Yields: 1½ cups

Ingredients:
⅔ cup organic rice milk, unsweetened
1 Tbsp. organic corn starch
¾ cup organic chicken stock
½ tsp. organic onion powder
½ tsp. organic black pepper
Dash of organic sea salt

Instructions:
Combine all ingredients in a sauce pan. Bring to a rapid boil, stirring constantly. Boil until soup thickens slightly. Cool and use in recipes as required.

***Variation 1:** For Cream of Celery Soup: Add ¼ cup of organic celery, washed and finely chopped. In a frying pan, sauté the celery in a dash of water until tender. Add to soup before bringing to a boil.

***Variation 2:** For Cream of Chicken Soup: Add ¼ cup of organic chicken, cooked and finely chopped. Add to soup before bringing to a boil.

***Variation 3:** For Cream of Mushroom Soup: Add ¼ cup of organic mushrooms, rinsed and finely chopped. In a frying pan, sauté the mushrooms in a dash of water until softened. Add to soup before bringing to a boil.

CREAMY POTATO SOUP

Preparation time: 20 minutes
Cook time: 4-5 hours
Serves: 5

Ingredients:
6 cups organic potatoes, peeled and diced
5 cups organic chicken broth
1 large organic onion, chopped
1 rib organic celery, chopped
2 organic carrots, chopped
¼ cup dairy and soy-free butter
2 tsp. organic sea salt
¼ tsp. organic black pepper
1½ cup organic rice milk, unsweetened

Instructions:
In a large crock pot, combine all ingredients and cook on high for 4-5 hours. Before serving, remove half of soup and puree in a food processor. Mix puree with original soup. Cool and serve with Fantastically Fluffy French Bread.*

*Variation 1: For Split Pea Soup: Soak 2 cups of organic split peas overnight. Substitute the split peas for the potatoes and puree as directed.

*See recipe for Fantastically Fluffy French Bread

GINGER SQUASH SOUP

Preparation time: 30 minutes
Cook time: 30 minutes
Serves: 5

Ingredients:
4 cups organic butternut squash (any winter squash)
2 Tbsp. dairy and soy-free cheese
¼ tsp. organic cinnamon
1 tsp. organic garlic powder
2 Tbsp. organic ground ginger
Dash of organic turmeric
Dash of organic nutmeg
2 Tbsp. organic clover honey
2 organic dried, pitted dates, finely chopped
5 cups water
1½ fresh organic orange juice (2 organic oranges)
¼ cup organic pumpkin seeds (optional topping)
½ cup organic plain coconut yogurt, unsweetened (optional topping)

Instructions:
Peel and juice two organic oranges. Set juice aside. In a medium sized pan, sauté squash and spices in butter until well-browned. Add water, honey, orange juice, and chopped dates. Bring mixture to a boil for 3 minutes. Cover. Reduce heat and simmer for 20 minutes or until squash has softened. Remove from heat and allow to cool slightly. Pour soup into a food processor and puree until very smooth. Return to pot and bring to a boil. Boil for 5 minutes. Reduce heat and simmer. Cool and serve with a dollop of plain coconut yogurt and a sprinkle of pumpkin seeds.

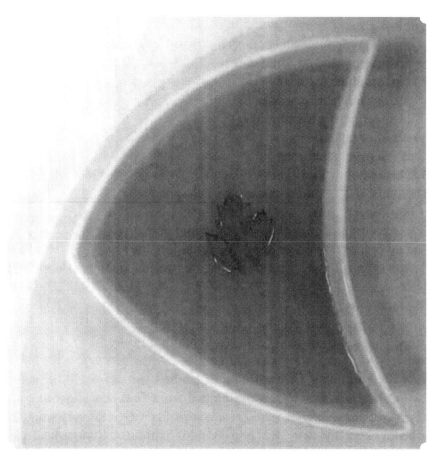

GINGER SQUASH SOUP

HEARTY BEEF STEW

Preparation time: 20 minutes
Cook time: 4-5 hours
Serves: 5

Ingredients:
Meat:
½ cup Knight's Nutritious GF Flour Blend
1 tsp. organic sea salt
¼ tsp. organic black pepper
2 lbs. organic beef stew meat, cubed in 1" pieces
2 Tbsp. dairy and soy-free butter

Broth:
6 cups organic beef broth
3 medium organic potatoes, peeled and cubed
4 organic carrots, diced
1 organic green pepper, diced
1 rib organic celery, diced
½ cup organic onion, chopped
1 Tbsp. organic sea salt
2 organic bay leaves

Instructions:
Meat preparation:
In a small bowl, combine flour, salt, and pepper. Toss beef in flour mixture until thoroughly coated. In a skillet, brown the floured beef in butter. In a large crock pot, combine all ingredients and browned meat. Cook on high for 5 hours. Serve with buttered Soft and Sweet Honey Bread.*

*See recipe for Soft and Sweet Honey Bread

ITALIAN VEGETABLE SOUP

Preparation time: 20 minutes
Cook time: 4-5 hours
Serves: 5

Ingredients:
1 lb. Italian Turkey Sausage*
1 Tbsp. extra virgin olive oil
1 cup organic onion, chopped
1 tsp. organic minced garlic
1 cup organic carrots, chopped
1 tsp. organic basil
2 small organic zucchinis, diced
1 (15 oz.) can organic diced tomatoes, undrained
1 tsp. organic sea salt
2½ cups organic beef broth
2 cups organic cabbage, shredded
1 tsp. organic Italian seasoning
¼ tsp. organic black pepper
1 (15 oz.) can organic great northern beans

Instructions:
Prepare 1 recipe of Italian Turkey Sausage. In a medium sized crock pot, combine cooked sausage and all ingredients and cook on high for 4-5 hours. Cool and serve.

*See recipe for Italian Turkey Sausage

TANGY TOMATO SOUP

Preparation time: 15 minutes
Cook time: 15 minutes
Serves: 5

Ingredients:
1 (28 oz.) can organic whole tomatoes, undrained
1½ cup organic chicken broth
½ cup organic rice milk, unsweetened
½ cup organic onion, diced
1 Tbsp. extra virgin olive oil
1 tsp. organic tomato paste
1 tsp. organic minced garlic
⅛ tsp. organic red pepper flakes
½ tsp. organic thyme
¼ tsp. organic basil
⅛ tsp. organic black pepper
⅛ tsp. organic sea salt
½ cup organic plain coconut yogurt, unsweetened (optional topping)
½ cup fresh basil (optional toppings)

Instructions:
In a medium pan, sauté onions and garlic in oil until tender and fragrant. Stir in tomato paste. Add in whole tomatoes, broth, and spices (except salt and pepper.) Stirring occasionally, simmer for 10 minutes. Add milk and simmer until tomatoes are very soft. Pour tomato mixture into a food processor and puree until smooth. Return to pan and bring to a boil stirring continually. Reduce heat and simmer. Serve with a dollop of yogurt, a sprinkle of fresh basil and well-buttered Herb Bread.*

*See recipe for Herb Bread

TURKEY SAUSAGE AND WHITE BEAN SOUP

Preparation time: 10 minutes
Cook time: 8 hours
Serves: 5

Ingredients:
1 lb. Italian Turkey Sausage*
2 (15 oz.) cans organic white beans
3 cups organic chicken broth
1 cup organic carrot, shredded
1 rib organic celery, finely chopped
1 Tbsp. extra virgin olive oil
3 tsp. organic minced garlic
1 tsp. organic marjoram
2 tsp. organic thyme
½ tsp. organic black pepper
1 tsp. organic sea salt

Instructions:
In a small frying pan, sauté the carrots and celery in olive oil until tender. Combine all ingredients in a large crock pot, cover, and cook on low for 8 hours. Serve with Sweet and Soft Honey Bread.*

*See recipe for Italian Turkey Sausage
*See recipe for Sweet and Soft Honey Bread

CHICKEN AND RED PEPPER SALAD

Preparation time: 10 minutes
Chill time: 30 minutes
Serves: 4

Ingredients:
2 free-range organic chicken breasts, cooked and cubed
¾ cup organic mayonnaise
½ cup fresh organic red pepper, chopped
¼ cup organic white onion, finely chopped
Dash of organic sea salt, to taste

Instructions:
In a small bowl, combine cubed chicken breast with mayonnaise and mix until chicken is covered with mayo. Add chopped peppers and onion. Stir until veggies are evenly distributed throughout. Season with sea salt. Chill for 30 minutes. Serve over lettuce or on Soft and Sweet Honey Bread.*

*See recipe for Soft and Sweet Honey Bread

EGG SALAD

Preparation time: 10 minutes
Chill time: 30 minutes
Yields: 2 cups

Ingredients:
10 cage-free organic eggs, hard boiled
¼-½ cup organic mayonnaise
1-1 ½ Tbsp. organic yellow mustard

Instructions:
Boil ten organic eggs in water containing ½ tsp. of baking soda to cause shells to come off more easily. Cube eggs and combine with all ingredients. Chill and serve on Delicious Dinner Rolls* or Soft and Sweet Honey Bread.*

*See recipe for Delicious Dinner Rolls
*See recipe for Soft and Sweet Honey Bread

POTATO SALAD

Preparation time: 20 minutes
Chill time: 30 minutes
Yields: 2 quarts

Ingredients:
4 medium organic potatoes, peeled and quartered
½ cup organic celery, chopped
¾ cup organic mayonnaise
2 Tbsp. organic rice milk, unsweetened
2 Tbsp. organic onion, chopped
1½ tsp. organic mustard
1 Tbsp. organic white vinegar
½ tsp. organic pickle juice
½ tsp. organic sea salt
½ tsp. organic black pepper

Instructions:
In a medium pot, boil peeled and quartered potatoes until soft. Chop celery and onion. Set aside. In a large mixing bowl combine wet ingredients and spices. Mix until well combined. Add vegetables. Drain potatoes and cut into bite sized pieces. Gently stir into sauce, being careful not to mash them. Cover and chill for 30 minutes. Serve and enjoy!

BACON BREAKFAST POTATOES

Preparation time: 15 minutes
Cook time: 10–15 minutes
Serves: 2

Ingredients:
2 tsp. extra virgin olive oil
2 small organic potatoes, peeled and cubed
2 organic carrot, shredded
¼ cup organic onion, finely chopped
¼ tsp. organic garlic salt
¼ lb. organic turkey bacon, cooked and chopped

Instructions:
Fry bacon to desired crispness. Cool and chop or tear into bite sized pieces. Set aside. In a skillet, sauté carrots and onions in a dash of oil over medium heat until tender. Add potatoes and cook until soft and lightly browned (about 10 minutes,) stirring occasionally. When potatoes are soft, add garlic salt and bacon. Heat thoroughly. Serve with freshly squeezed organic orange juice.

BAKED ROSEMARY POTATOES

Preparation time: 10 minutes
Cook time: 30 minutes
Serves: 6

Ingredients:
6 organic potatoes, cubed
¼ cup organic onion, finely diced
¼ cup organic carrot, shredded
5 Tbsp. extra virgin olive oil
1½ tsp. organic garlic salt
¾ tsp. organic black pepper
2 tsp. organic rosemary
2 tsp. organic thyme
2 tsp. organic herbs province
Dash of organic garlic powder

Instructions:
Scrub and cube potatoes, leaving the skins on. Set aside. In a small skillet, sauté onion and carrot in 1 Tbsp. of olive oil. Spread 1 Tbsp. of oil over bottom of baking sheet. Sprinkle pan with ½ tsp. of garlic salt. Place potato pieces on baking sheet and drizzle with remaining oil. Sprinkle with spices and toss potatoes until all are covered with oil and seasonings. Bake for 15 minutes then rotate the potatoes. Bake for an additional 10-15 minutes or until lightly crispy. Serve and enjoy!

BAKED ROSEMARY POTATOES

CABBAGE KRAUT BURGERS

Preparation time: 15 minutes
Cook time: 3-4 hours
Yields: 12

Ingredients:
Filling:
1 lb. free-range organic ground turkey, fried
½ cup organic onion, chopped
1 lb. organic cabbage, shredded
1-2 organic carrots, grated
1 tsp. organic sea salt
3 cups dairy and soy-free cheese, reserve

Bun:
Prepare one recipe of Fantastically Fluffy French Bread.* Separate into 12 equal parts and set aside.

Instructions:

Preheat oven to 350 degrees.

Butter a baking sheet and set aside.

In medium sized skillet, fry ground turkey, drain, and set aside. Sauté onion and carrots in a dash of water until tender. Add cabbage. Cover and cook until cabbage softens. Add browned meat and season with salt.

To form burgers, sprinkle a teaspoon of flour in the base of a soup bowl. Lightly butter sides of bowl, but not to top rim. Dust one piece of prepared dough with flour. Using a floured rolling pin, gently flatten dough into a circle. Transfer flattened dough to prepared bowl. Place ¼ cup of meat and cabbage mixture on dough. Top with a ⅛ cup of cheese. Using fingers, gather edges of dough and pinch together to close burger. Flip bowl over and deposit burger onto buttered baking sheet. Prepare all burgers and bake for 25 minutes or until tops are lightly brown. Dip in Balsamic Salad Dressing.*

*See recipe for Fantastically Fluffy French Bread
*See recipe for Balsamic Salad Dressing

CAULIFLOWER PIZZA CRUST

Preparation time: 15 minutes
Cook time: 15–20 minutes
Yields: 1

Ingredients:
2-3 cups Riced Cauliflower,* very dry
⅓ cup dairy and soy-free cheese
1 cage-free organic egg, beaten
⅛ tsp. organic savory
½ tsp. organic herbs province
½ tsp. organic fennel seeds
⅛ tsp. organic sea salt
⅛ tsp. organic black pepper
1 Tbsp. organic Italian seasoning

Instructions:
Preheat oven to 450 degrees.
Line a baking sheet with a layer of parchment paper. In a medium sized bowl, mix very dry cauliflower rice with egg, cheese, and spices until well combined. Place cauliflower dough onto parchment paper. Flatten to desired shape and thickness. Bake for 15–20 minutes or until lightly browned. Remove from oven and top with sauce, cheese, vegetables, organic pre-cooked turkey bacon (chopped,) and Italian Turkey Sausage.* Bake pizza for 10-15 minutes or until cheese has thoroughly melted.

*See recipe for Riced Cauliflower
*See recipe for Italian Turkey Sausage

GARLIC SPAGHETTI SQUASH

Preparation time: 10 minutes
Cook time: 30 minutes
Serves: 2

Ingredients:
2-3 lbs. boiled spaghetti squash (see instructions below)
2 Tbsp. dairy and soy-free butter
1 Tbsp. organic minced garlic
1-2 Tbsp. organic parsley
1-2 Tbsp. organic basil
Dash of organic sea salt, to taste
¼ cup dairy and soy-free cheese, chopped (optional)

Instructions:
Boiled Squash:
Fill large pot half full of water and bring to a rapid boil. Cut spaghetti squash into quarters and spoon out seeds. Place squash quarters in water and boil for 15 minutes. When thoroughly cooked, remove from water and cool. Using a fork or spoon, scrape the stringy squash from the skin and place in a separate bowl.

In a medium sized skillet, sauté garlic in butter until tender and savory. Add squash and season to taste with parsley, basil, and salt. Stir in cheese and allow to melt thoroughly. Do not overcook. Squash should maintain a slightly crunchy texture. Serve and enjoy!

*Variation 1: For Garlic Chicken Squash: Add in one cooked chicken breast (cubed) seasoned with garlic salt and oil.

GARLIC SPAGHETTI SQUASH

GRILLED BROCCOLI

Preparation time: 5 minutes
Cook time: 5 minutes
Serves: 4

Ingredients:
2 heads fresh organic broccoli
2 Tbsp. extra virgin olive oil
½ tsp. organic sea salt

Instructions:
Wash and cut fresh broccoli into small or medium sized pieces with long stems. In a large bowl, toss broccoli in oil and salt until florets are thoroughly covered. Place broccoli in a medium sized frying pan and cook until florets are tender (about 5 minutes.) Serve as a side dish.

MASHED CAULIFLOWER

Preparation time: 30 minutes
Cook time: 20 minutes
Serves: 3

Ingredients:
2 heads organic cauliflower, washed, cut in large pieces
2 Tbsp. diary and soy-free butter
½ tsp. organic sea salt

Instructions:
Preheat oven to 350 degrees.
Steam cauliflower until tender. Puree cauliflower in food processer. Place in a bowl. Add butter and salt and blend until smooth. Pour the cauliflower into an 8x8 glass dish and heat in the oven for 20 minutes or until peaks become lightly browned. Cool, serve and enjoy!

MASHED POTATOES

Preparation time: 15 minutes
Cook time: 10 minutes
Serves: 2

Ingredients:
4 large organic potatoes, peeled and cubed
½ cup dairy and soy-free butter
½ cup organic rice milk, unsweetened

Instructions:
Fill a medium sized pot half full of water and bring to a rapid boil. Peel and cube potatoes. Boil the potatoes for 10 minutes or until they are soft but not mushy. Drain and return potatoes to pot. Mash the potatoes using a potato masher. Add butter and milk and blend until soft and fluffy using a hand mixer. Serve as a side dish.

*Variation 1: For Garlic Mashed Potatoes: Add in 1 tsp. of organic garlic powder and a dash of organic parsley.

RICED CAULIFLOWER

Preparation time: 1-2 hours
Cook time: 20-28 minutes
Yields: 4 cups

Ingredients:
1 head of organic cauliflower

Instructions:
Cut cauliflower into florets, removing the leaves and the hard core. Gently rinse the florets. Place on a clean towel to dry completely (1-2 hours.) *The cauliflower must be completely dry before ricing.* When the florets are dry, place ⅓ of them into the food processor and chop into rice sized pieces. Remove the rice and continue to process the remaining florets.

Preheat oven to 375 degrees.
Place the rice in an 8x8 glass pan. Cover and bake for 20-28 minutes or until dry but not browned. Serve alone or use as a recipe base.

ROAST ASPARAGUS

Preparation time: 5 minutes
Cook time: 10-12 minutes
Serves: 4

Ingredients:
1 fresh organic asparagus bunch, washed
2 Tbsp. extra virgin olive oil
¼-½ tsp. organic sea salt

Instructions:
Preheat oven to 350 degrees.
Trim ½ inch from the bottom of each asparagus stalk. Line a 9x13 pan with asparagus stalks, drizzle with olive oil, and roll stalks over to ensure that each stalk is completely covered in oil. Salt to taste and roast for 10-12 minutes or until tips are lightly browned. Serve as a side dish.

DRESSINGS, SAUCES & SEASONINGS

ASSORTED SPICES

DRESSINGS, SAUCES & SEASONINGS

ALTERNATIVE GLUTEN-FREE SOY SAUCE

Preparation time: 5 minutes
Cook time: 15 minutes
Yields: 1 cup

Ingredients:
4 tsp. organic balsamic vinegar
1 tsp. organic apple cider vinegar
2 tsp. unsulphured black strap molasses
¼ tsp. organic ground ginger
1½ cups organic beef broth
Dash of organic black pepper
Dash of organic garlic powder
Dash of organic sea salt, to taste

Instructions:
In a sauce pan, combine all ingredients and bring a light boil. Reduce heat and simmer for 15 minutes. Cool and season with salt, to taste. Store in a sealed container in refrigerator for up to 1 week. Use this alternative sauce in any recipe that calls for soy sauce.

BALSAMIC MARINADE

Preparation time: 5 minutes
Cook time: 0 minutes
Yields: ¼ cup

Ingredients:
3 tsp. organic balsamic vinegar
3 tsp. organic clover honey
2 tsp. organic yellow mustard
¾ tsp. organic sesame oil
Dash of organic sea salt

Instructions:
In a small bowl, combine all ingredients and mix until thoroughly blended. Use marinade as a sauce, dressing, or seasoning.

BALSAMIC SALAD DRESSING

Preparation time: 5 minutes
Chill time: 20 minutes
Serves: 4

Ingredients:
¾ cup organic balsamic vinegar
1 tsp. extra virgin olive oil
1 Tbsp. organic lemon juice
3 Tbsp. organic yellow mustard
2 tsp. fresh organic basil
2 tsp. fresh organic onion, finely chopped
Dash of organic sea salt, to taste
Dash of organic black pepper

Instructions:
In a small bowl, combine all ingredients and mix thoroughly. Cover and chill for 20 minutes. Serve over salad.

BASIC KETCHUP

Preparation time: 15 minutes
Chill time: 4 hours
Yields: 2 cups

Ingredients:
1 (9 oz.) can organic tomato paste
3 Tbsp. organic white vinegar
½ tsp. organic garlic powder
1½ tsp. organic onion powder
1 Tbsp. organic clover honey
1 Tbsp. unsulphured black strap molasses
½ tsp. organic sea salt
½ tsp. organic yellow mustard
⅛ tsp. organic cinnamon
⅛ tsp. organic ground cloves
⅛ tsp. organic turmeric
⅛ tsp organic cayenne
½ cup water

Instructions:
Combine all ingredients in a food processor and mix until thoroughly combined. Cover and chill for 4 hours or over-night. Serve and enjoy!

BASIL SALAD DRESSING

Preparation time: 5 minutes
Cook time: 5 minutes
Yields: 2 cups

Ingredients:
1 Tbsp. organic thyme
2 Tbsp. organic garlic salt
4 Tbsp. organic basil
1⅛ cup extra virgin olive oil

Instructions:
In a small sauce pan, combine all ingredients over medium heat. Stir until garlic salt is completely dissolved. Cool completely and serve over fresh salad.

BASIL SALAD DRESSING

CACCIATORE SAUCE

Preparation time: 10 minutes
Cook time: 3-4 hours
Serves: 5

Ingredients:
1 tsp. organic sea salt
¼ tsp. organic black pepper
2 tsp. organic oregano
½ tsp. organic red pepper flakes
1 Tbsp. extra virgin olive oil
1 organic red pepper, chopped
1 organic green pepper, chopped
1 small organic onion, chopped
2 Tbsp. organic minced garlic
2 (15 oz.) cans organic tomatoes, diced
1 cup organic chicken broth
1 tsp. organic parsley
1 tsp. organic basil
½ cup Knight's Nutritious GF Flour Blend

Instructions:
In a medium sized crock pot, combine all ingredients and cook on high for 3-4 hours. Use in any recipe that calls for cacciatore sauce.

CAESAR SALAD DRESSING

Preparation time: 5 minutes
Cook time: 0 minutes
Yields: 1 cup

Ingredients:
1 cup organic mayonnaise
1 Tbsp. organic plain coconut yogurt, unsweetened
2 tsp. organic lemon juice
2 tsp. Homemade Worcestershire Sauce*
1 tsp. organic garlic powder
¼ tsp. organic sea salt
⅛ tsp. organic black pepper
⅓ cup dairy and soy-free cheese, finely chopped
½ tsp. organic Dijon mustard
Dash of water (if needed to loosen the consistency)

Instructions:
In a small bowl, combine all ingredients and blend until a smooth texture is achieved. Add water to attain desired consistency. Cover in a sealed container and store in the refrigerator for up to 1 week.

*See recipe for Homemade Worcestershire Sauce

CONCENTRATED COCONUT MILK

Preparation time: 5 minutes
Cook time: 40 minutes
Yields: 15 ounces

Ingredients:
1 (15 oz.) can organic, full-fat coconut milk, unsweetened
⅛ cup organic clover honey
⅛ cup agave nectar
½ tsp. pure organic vanilla extract (optional)

Instructions:
Pour the full-fat milk and vanilla (optional) into a medium sized pan and bring to a rapid boil, stirring constantly. Allow the milk to boil for 4-5 minutes. Reduce heat and bring to a simmer. Add honey and agave. Stir simmering mixture until it is smooth. Continue to simmer mixture over low heat for 40 minutes or until liquid has decreased to a condensed state. Stir often. Cool and cover the milk in a sealed container until needed. Refrigerate for up to 1 week.

CROCKPOT CINNAMON APPLESAUCE

Preparation time: 5 minutes
Cook time: 5 hours
Yields: 4½ cups

Ingredients:
10 large organic apples, peeled and thinly sliced
½ cup water
¼ cup organic clover honey
2 tsp. organic cinnamon
1 Tbsp. organic lemon juice

Instructions:
Peel and slice apples and set aside.
In a large crock pot, combine all ingredients and toss in apples. Cover and cook on low for 5 hours or until apples are soupy. Cool. In a food processor, blend the sauce until smooth. Place in a sealed container and store in the refrigerator for up to 2 weeks.

HERB GRAVY

Preparation time: 10 minutes
Cook time: 5 minutes
Serves: 8 cups

Ingredients:
1 qt. organic chicken stock
2 tsp. organic garlic powder
½ tsp. organic black pepper, to taste
½ tsp. organic sea salt, to taste
1 Tbsp. organic thyme
2 tsp. organic herbs province
T Tbsp. organic poultry seasoning
1 tsp. organic onion powder
½ cup organic cornstarch
Organic pan drippings from chicken or turkey (up to 4 cups)

Instructions:
In a frying pan, sauté the garlic, onion, and oil until fragrant. In a separate bowl, combine the stock and corn starch and mix until the starch has completely dissolved. Pour the starch mixture into the frying pan and add the drippings. Bring the mixture to a slow boil, stirring continuously until the liquid thickens into gravy. Season to taste with spices, salt and pepper. Serve and enjoy!

HOMEMADE WORCESTERSHIRE SAUCE

Preparation time: 5 minutes
Cook time: 0 minutes
Yields: ¾ cup

Ingredients:
⅓ cup organic apple cider vinegar
2 Tbsp. organic clover honey
1 tsp. unsulphured black strap molasses
1 tsp. organic lemon juice
½ tsp. organic ground cloves
½ tsp. organic onion powder
¼ tsp. organic garlic powder
¼ tsp. organic chili powder

Instructions:
Combine all ingredients in a small bowl and mix well. Place the sauce in a sealed container and refrigerate for up to 1 month. Use this sauce as a substitute in any recipe that calls for Worcestershire sauce.

HOMEMADE WORCESTERSHIRE SAUCE
& PUNGENT HERB DRESSING

HOT TACO SEASONING

Preparation time: 3 minutes
Cook time: 0 minutes
Yields: ½ cup

Ingredients:
2 Tbsp. organic chili powder
½ Tbsp. organic black pepper
½ Tbsp. organic garlic powder
1 tsp. organic cumin
1 tsp. organic turmeric
1 tsp. organic oregano
⅛ tsp. organic cayenne pepper
⅛ tsp. organic red pepper flakes
Dash of organic sea salt

Instructions:
Combine all ingredients and use immediately or store indefinitely in a sealed container.

MILD TACO SEASONING

Preparation time: 5 minutes
Cook time: 0 minutes
Yields: ½ cup

Ingredients:
2 tsp. organic chili powder
1½ tsp. organic minced onion
1 tsp. organic sea salt
1 tsp. organic paprika
¼ tsp. organic cayenne pepper
¼ tsp. organic garlic powder
¼ tsp. organic onion powder
¼ tsp. organic cumin

Instructions:
Mix together and use immediately or store indefinitely in a sealed container.

MOUTH-WATERING BARBECUE SAUCE

Preparation time: 5 minutes
Chill time: 20 minutes
Serves: 5

Ingredients:
¼ cup Basic Ketchup*
2 tsp. organic garlic powder
½ tsp. organic agave nectar
2 tsp. organic yellow mustard
1 Tbsp. organic apple cider vinegar
2 Tbsp. Homemade Worcestershire Sauce*
¼ cup organic tomato sauce
¼ tsp. organic all spice
Dash of organic cayenne pepper

Instructions:
Combine all ingredients in a small bowl and mix thoroughly. Refrigerate for at least 2 hours to set the flavor. Use this sauce as a condiment or in any recipe where barbeque sauce is required.

*See recipe for Basic Ketchup
*See recipe for Homemade Worcestershire Sauce

ORANGE DRESSING

Preparation time: 5 minutes
Chill time: 20 minutes
Yields: ¾ cup

Ingredients:
½ cup fresh, organic orange juice (1 organic orange)
2 Tbsp. organic apple cider vinegar
2 Tbsp. extra virgin olive oil
2 tsp. organic garlic powder
Dash of organic orange zest

Instructions:
In a small bowl, combine all ingredients and mix well. Cover and refrigerate for 20 minutes. Serve over salad.

PIZZA SAUCE

Preparation time: 10 minutes
Cook time: 30 minutes
Yields: 20 ounces

Ingredients:
1 (15 oz.) can organic tomato sauce
2 (6 oz.) cans organic tomato paste
2 Tbsp. extra virgin olive oil
2 Tbsp. organic dairy and soy-free butter
¾ cup organic onion, chopped
2 tsp. organic garlic powder
1 tsp. organic paprika
2 tsp. organic basil
2 tsp. organic oregano
2 tsp. organic fennel seeds
1 tsp. organic sea salt
½ tsp. organic black pepper
2 organic bay leaves

Instructions:
In a frying pan, sauté onion and garlic in oil and butter until tender. Puree onion, garlic, tomato sauce, and tomato paste in a food processor until smooth. Pour back into pan and add in remaining ingredients. Simmer sauce over low heat for 30 minutes. Remove the bay leaf. Use the sauce in any recipe that calls for pizza sauce.

Hint: Freeze remaining sauce in a sealed freezer-safe container or bag.

PUNGENT HERB DRESSING

Preparation time: 10 minutes
Chill time: 30 minutes
Yields: 1 cup

Ingredients:
1 cup organic, full-fat coconut milk, unsweetened
½ Tbsp. organic yellow mustard
½ tsp. organic paprika
¼ tsp. organic dried dill
⅛ tsp. organic celery seeds
½ Tbsp. organic parsley
½ tsp. organic garlic powder
¼ tsp. organic onion powder
¼ tsp. organic black pepper
½ tsp. organic sea salt
Dash of organic turmeric

Instructions:
In a medium sized bowl, combine milk and spices. Blend until smooth and refrigerate for at least 30 minutes. Serve over organic vegetable salad or as a vegetable dip.

*Variation 1: For White Ranch Dressing: Remove the turmeric, paprika, and mustard for a creamier and less tangy dressing. Chill and serve.

RICH APPLE BUTTER

Preparation time: 30 minutes
Cook time: 3 hours & 20 minutes
Yields: 32 ounces

Ingredients:
12 organic apples, peeled and chopped
1½ cups organic apple cider vinegar
1 cup pure organic maple syrup
½ cup unsulphured black strap molasses
2 Tbsp. fresh organic lemon juice
3 tsp. organic ground cinnamon
3 tsp. organic pure vanilla extract
½ tsp. organic ground cloves
½ tsp. organic nutmeg
1 tsp. organic sea salt

Instructions:
In a large pot, combine the apples, cider, syrup, molasses, and sea salt. Simmer over medium heat for 15-20 minutes. When the apples are soft, remove the mixture from heat and stir in the cinnamon, vanilla, cloves, nutmeg, and lemon juice. When it has cooled, pour it into a food processor and puree it. Next, pour the pureed sauce into an uncovered steel pan and bake it for approximately 3 hours. Stir it every 30 minutes until it thickens and the color turns to a deep brown. Cool completely. Place the sauce in a sealed glass jar and refrigerate for up to 2 weeks.

RICH APPLE BUTTER

SPICY CUMIN SALAD DRESSING

Preparation time: 10 minutes
Chill time: 20 minutes
Serves: 2

Ingredients:
1 Tbsp. extra virgin olive oil
½ Tbsp. organic yellow mustard
½ fresh orange juice (1 organic orange)
2 Tbsp. fresh organic lemon juice
½ tsp. organic ground cumin
⅛ tsp. organic black pepper
¼ tsp. organic sea salt
Dash of organic turmeric

Instructions:
In a small bowl, mix all the ingredients until smooth. Chill for 20 minutes and serve over salad or as a vegetable dip.

ZESTY SALSA

Preparation time: 15 minutes
Cook time: 15 minutes
Yields: 3 cups

Ingredients:
1 (28 oz.) can organic whole tomatoes, drained
2 cups fresh, organic onion, diced
3 tsp. organic minced garlic
1-2 tsp. organic garlic powder, to taste
2 organic habanero peppers, seeded and halved
½ cup fresh organic leaks, diced
¼ cup fresh organic oregano
1 cup fresh organic cilantro
½ tsp. organic sea salt
1 Tbsp. extra virgin olive oil
½ tsp. organic cumin
1 tsp. organic lemon juice (optional)
¼ tsp. organic red pepper flakes (optional)
Dash of organic ground pepper

Instructions:
In a food processor, puree the tomatoes, cilantro, and peppers until smooth. Set aside. In a large skillet, sauté the onions and garlic in oil until tender and fragrant. Pour tomato puree into skillet and stir until thoroughly combined. Season to taste with salt, pepper, cumin, and garlic powder. Simmer over low heat until it begins to thicken. If the salsa is too spicy, soften it with one teaspoon of lemon juice. If salsa is not spicy enough, season with ¼ teaspoon of red pepper flakes. Cool and serve over organic Mexican food or with organic corn chips.

PASTA, RICE & BEANS

MEAT LOVER'S LASAGNA

PASTA, RICE & BEANS

CHICKEN CALIENTE CASSEROLE

Preparation time: 10 minutes
Cook time: 10 minutes
Serves: 5

Ingredients
2 cups free-range organic chicken, cooked and cubed
1 (8 oz.) package organic gluten-free rice noodles
1 (15 oz.) can organic great northern beans, drained
¼ cup Mild Taco Seasoning*
¼ cup organic cayenne pepper
1 cup organic dairy and soy-free cheese, grated
2 recipes Cream of Chicken Soup*

Instructions:
Fill a medium size pan with water and bring to a boil. Add noodles and cook according to package directions. Drain and set aside. In a small sauce pan over low heat, combine soup, seasoning, cayenne, and cheese. Heat until cheese is melted and mixture is warm. Add the noodles and beans to the cheese mixture. Stir until noodles are evenly covered with the cheese sauce. Serve and enjoy!

*See recipe for Cream of Chicken Soup
*See recipe for Mild Taco Seasoning

CHUNKY CHILI

Preparation time: 25 minutes
Cook time: 15 minutes
Serves: 5

Ingredients:
1 lb. organic free-range ground beef, browned
1 (45 oz.) can organic stewed tomatoes, undrained
1 (15 oz.) can organic tomato sauce
1 (15 oz.) can organic chili beans, drained
1 cup fresh organic onion, chopped
¼ tsp. organic garlic powder
1 tsp. organic paprika
2 Tbsp. organic chili powder
½ tsp. organic sea salt
1 tsp. Homemade Worcestershire Sauce*
1 tsp. organic red pepper flakes

Instructions:
In a large skillet, brown the hamburger. Drain it set it aside. Add a thin layer of water to the skillet and sauté the onions and garlic until tender and fragrant. Combine all the ingredients in a large pot. Bring the chili to a slow boil and cook for 10-15 minutes or until ingredients are well combined and the beans are soft. Serve with corn chips or Golden Corn Bread.*

*See recipe for Homemade Worcestershire Sauce
*See recipe for Golden Corn Bread

CHUNKY CHILI

MEAT LOVER'S LASAGNA

Preparation time: 45 minutes
Cook time: 45 minutes
Serves: 6

Ingredients:
1 lb. organic ground turkey, browned
1 lb. organic ground beef, browned
1 (10 oz.) package oven-ready, gluten-free lasagna noodles
2 (15 oz.) cans organic diced tomatoes, drained
2 (15 oz.) cans organic tomato sauce
1 (4 oz.) can organic green chilies
1 (10 oz.) bag dairy and soy-free cheese
3 tsp. organic minced garlic
3 tsp. organic garlic powder
4 tsp. organic ground thyme
2 Tbsp. organic herbs province
1 tsp. organic savory
2 Tbsp. organic oregano
1 Tbsp. organic parsley
1 Tbsp. organic fennel
2 Tbsp. organic basil
½ cup organic Italian seasoning
2 tsp. organic sea salt
¼ cup Italian seasoning, reserve
2 tsp. garlic powder, reserve

*Increase any spice to taste

Instructions:

In a large frying pan, brown the turkey and beef together. Drain the meat and set it aside. Add a dash of water to the frying pan and sauté the garlic until it becomes fragrant. Add in the tomato sauce, diced tomatoes, and green chilies. Stir well and toss in the remaining seasonings. (Adjust spice amounts to achieve desired taste.) When the sauce is well seasoned, simmer it over medium heat for 30 minutes. Stir in the browned meat.

Place one layer of oven-ready noodles in the bottom of a 9x13 pan. Spread half of the meat mixture over the noodles and sprinkle it with an ⅛ cup of Italian seasoning, 1 teaspoon of garlic powder, and a dash of sea salt. Cover this with a thick layer of cheese. Layer the remaining noodles over the meat and cheese. Spread the remaining meat mixture over noodles and sprinkle it with the left over Italian seasoning, garlic powder, and sea salt. Finally, spread a thin layer of cheese over the top. Lightly pat the cheese down into the meat. Cover and refrigerate the lasagna for at least 2 hours. For best results, cover and refrigerate the lasagna overnight. When ready to cook, preheat the oven to 350 degrees and bake the lasagna for 45 minutes or until the cheese has melted throughout.

MEXICAN BEAN DIP

Preparation time: 20 minutes
Cook time: 5 minutes
Serves: 5

Ingredients:
4 organic jalapeno peppers, chopped (optional)
¼ cup organic Hot Taco Seasoning*
1 (24 oz.) organic refried beans
1 lb. organic free-range ground beef, browned
¼ tsp. organic cayenne pepper
1 cup Zesty Salsa*

Instructions:
In a large skillet, brown the hamburger, drain, and set aside. Place a ¼ cup of water in the skillet and add the taco seasoning, cayenne pepper and chopped jalapeno peppers. Simmer for 30 seconds. Add the refried beans and salsa. Stir in the hamburger and heat the dip thoroughly. Serve with guacamole and corn chips or in Tender Tortillas.*

*See recipe for Hot Taco Seasoning
*See recipe for Zesty Salsa
*See recipe for Tender Tortillas

MILD CHICKEN FRIED RICE

Preparation time: 10 minutes
Cook time: 10 minutes
Serves: 4

Ingredients:
1 lb. organic free-range chicken, cooked, cubed
2 Tbsp. Alternative Gluten-Free Soy Sauce*
½-1 tsp. organic corn starch (to thicken sauce)
½ Tbsp. organic sesame oil
1 cup fresh organic onion, finely chopped
1 organic carrot, chopped
1 rib organic celery, finely chopped
½ cup organic fresh red bell pepper, chopped (optional)
½ cup organic fresh peas (optional)
4 cups organic brown rice, cooked
1 tsp. organic dairy and soy-free butter
2 organic cage-free eggs, scrambled
Dash of organic garlic powder
Dash of organic sea salt, to taste
Dash of organic black pepper, to taste

Instructions:

Prepare the rice and scrambled eggs and set aside.

In a large skillet, sauté the onions and garlic powder in sesame oil until tender. Add in the cubed chicken and 1 Tbsp. of soy sauce. Fry for 3 minutes. Toss in the vegetables and butter. Fry for another 4 minutes. Add in the rice and the last Tbsp. of soy sauce. Stir thoroughly and toss in the scrambled eggs. Season with salt and pepper. Heat the rice thoroughly. Serve and enjoy!

*Variation 1: For Turkey Bacon Fried Rice: Substitute 1lb. of turkey bacon for the chicken.

*See recipe for Alternative Gluten-Free Soy Sauce

RAISIN RICE PORRIDGE

Preparation time: 10 minutes
Cook time: 4-6 hours
Serves: 4

Ingredients:
⅔ cup organic brown rice, uncooked
⅛ tsp. organic sea salt
¼ cup organic agave
1¾ cup organic coconut milk, unsweetened
¼ tsp. organic nutmeg
¼ tsp. organic cinnamon
½ tsp. organic pure vanilla extract
½ Tbsp. organic dairy and soy-free butter
½ cup organic raisins, unsweetened
¼ cup unsweetened, dried organic fruit (optional)

Instructions:
Thoroughly butter a 1½ quart crock pot. Mix the rice, salt, nutmeg, and cinnamon together in a bowl and pour it into the crock pot. Add in the milk, agave, butter, and fruit (optional) and stir to combine. Cook on high until the porridge reaches a steady boil (3-4 hours.) Reduce the heat to low and simmer the mixture until the rice absorbs the moisture and it doubles in size (1 hour.) Cool, serve and enjoy!

RAISIN RICE PORRIDGE

SPAGHETTI

Preparation time: 15 minutes
Cook time: 10 minutes
Serves: 2

Ingredients:
1 lb. free-range organic ground beef, browned
¼ cup fresh organic onion, chopped
¼ cup organic mushrooms, chopped
1 tsp. organic garlic salt
2 tsp. extra virgin olive oil
1 (24 oz.) can organic spaghetti sauce
1 (10 oz.) box gluten-free spaghetti noodles, boiled

Instructions:
Prepare noodles according to package directions. In a frying pan, sauté the onions and mushrooms in dash of oil until tender and fragrant. Set aside in a separate dish. In the frying pan, brown the hamburger, drain it and return it to the pan. Add in the sautéed vegetables, sauce, and seasoning. Bring to a slow bowl. Reduce the heat and cool. Serve the sauce over the spaghetti noodles with a side of steamed vegetables.

SPANISH RICE

Preparation time: 45 minutes
Cook time: 5 minutes
Serves: 5

Ingredients:
1 lb. free-range organic ground beef, browned
1 small organic onion, chopped
2 tsp. organic minced garlic
4 cups organic brown rice, cooked
1 (15 oz.) can organic tomato sauce
1 Tbsp. organic chili powder
½ tsp. organic cayenne
½ tsp. organic cumin
1 tsp. organic red pepper flakes

Instructions:
Prepare the brown rice and set it aside. In a medium sized skillet, brown the beef, drain it, and set it aside. In a frying pan, sauté the onions and garlic in dash of water until tender and fragrant. Combine the tomato sauce, seasoning, meat, and rice. Warm the mixture thoroughly. Serve and enjoy!

BEEF, POULTRY, FISH & EGG

BASIL CHICKEN

BEEF, POULTRY, FISH & EGG

BAKED SALMON WITH BALSAMIC MARINADE

Preparation time: 5 minutes
Cook time: 15 minutes
Serves: 2

Ingredients:
1 (12 oz.) fresh water salmon fillet, raw
2 recipes Balsamic Marinade*
1 recipe Roast Asparagus*

Instructions:
Marinade salmon fillet in the Balsamic Marinade and cover for 2 hours. Preheat oven to 450 degrees. Bake the fillet for 15 minutes or until the salmon becomes slightly flaky. Cool and serve with Roast Asparagus.

*See recipe for Balsamic Marinade
*See recipe for Roast Asparagus

BASIL CHICKEN

Preparation time: 10 minutes
Cook time: 30-35 minutes
Serves: 4

Ingredients:
4 free-range organic chicken breasts, raw
1½ tsp. organic thyme
3 tsp. organic garlic salt
2 Tbsp. organic basil
9 Tbsp. extra virgin olive oil

Instructions:
Place the raw chicken breast in 9x13 pan. In a small bowl, combine thyme, salt, basil, and oil. Mix to combine. While stirring, pour the sauce evenly over the chicken. For best results, cover and refrigerate the chicken for 4 hours prior to baking. When ready to bake, preheat oven to 400 degrees. Bake chicken for 30-35 minutes or until juice runs clear. Reserve juices/sauce and pour it over rice or potatoes. Serve with cooked vegetables.

CHICKEN A LA KING

Preparation time: 10 minutes
Cook time: 4-5 hours
Serves: 5

Ingredients:
1 recipe Cream of Chicken Soup*
3 Tbsp. Knight's Nutritious GF Flour Blend
¼ tsp. organic black pepper
¼ tsp. organic cayenne pepper
3 cups free-range organic chicken breast, cooked and cubed
1 rib organic celery, chopped
1 organic green pepper, chopped
½ cup organic onion, chopped
2 Tbsp. organic pimentos, drained
1 cup organic brown rice, uncooked
1½ cups water

Instructions:
In a large crock pot, combine all ingredients and cook on high for 3-4 hours. Serve with Dad's Fluffy Biscuits,* or with Fantastically Fluffy French Bread.*

*See recipe for Cream of Chicken Soup
*See recipe for Dad's Fluffy Biscuits
*See recipe for Fantastically Fluffy French Bread

CHICKEN FAJITAS

Preparation time: 15 minutes
Cook time: 10 minutes
Serves: 4

Ingredients:
2 free-range organic chicken breasts, cooked and chopped
1 medium organic onion, chopped
2 tsp. organic minced garlic
1 (6 oz.) can organic tomato sauce
1 tsp. organic chili powder
¼ tsp. organic black pepper
½ tsp. organic sea salt
1 tsp. organic lemon juice

Instructions:
In a frying pan, sauté the onions and garlic in a dash of water until tender. Add in the cooked chicken and remaining ingredients. Simmer over medium heat until it is completely warm throughout. Serve over rice, GF noodles, or in Tender Tortillas.*

*See recipe for Tender Tortillas

CHICKEN NOODLE CASSEROLE

Preparation time: 15 minutes
Cook time: 10 minutes
Serves: 5

Ingredients:
2 cups gluten-free noodles, boiled and drained
3 cups free-range organic chicken breasts, cooked and chopped
2 recipes Cream of Chicken Soup*
1 tsp. organic sea salt
2 tsp. organic poultry seasoning
1 cup dairy and soy-free cheese
1½ tsp. organic prepared mustard
¼ cup organic chopped mushrooms (optional)

Instructions:
In a small pot, cook the noodles according to the package instructions. Drain them and set them aside. Prepare the soup and set aside. In a medium sized skillet, combine the chicken, soup, spices, cheese and mustard. Stir in the noodles and completely coat them with the cheese sauce. Warm the casserole over medium heat. Serve with a side of steamed vegetables.

*See recipe for Cream of Chicken Soup

DESERT CACTUS MEATBALLS

Preparation time: 30 minutes
Cook time: 1 hour
Serves: 5

Ingredients:
Meatballs:
1 lb. free-range organic ground beef, raw
½ cup organic brown rice, uncooked
½ cup water
⅓ cup fresh organic onion, finely chopped
1 tsp. organic sea salt
½ tsp. organic celery seed
⅛ tsp. organic garlic powder
⅛ tsp. organic black pepper

Sauce:
1 (15 oz.) can organic tomato sauce
1 cup water
2 tsp. Homemade Worcestershire Sauce*

Instructions:
In a large bowl, combine all the meatball ingredients and mix well. Roll the meat mixture into 1 inch meatballs, brown them in a skillet, and place them in a large crock pot. In a separate bowl, mix the sauce ingredients and pour it over the meatballs. Cover and cook on high for 3-4 hours. Serve over Mashed Potatoes* or brown rice.

*See recipe for Homemade Worcestershire Sauce
*See recipe for Mashed Potatoes

DUTCH OVEN ROASTED CHICKEN

Preparation time: 15 minutes
Cook time: 1½ hours
Serves: 5

Ingredients:
1 small or medium free-range, organic whole chicken
1 organic lemon, halved
1 head organic garlic, crushed
2 Tbsp. extra virgin olive oil
1 small organic onion, quartered
1½ cups fresh organic thyme
¼ cup dairy and soy-free butter

Instructions:
Preheat oven to 425 degrees.
Remove the giblets from the chicken and rinse out the chicken thoroughly. Place the chicken in an 8 quart Dutch oven and add a ½ inch of water to the bottom of the pan. Generously salt and pepper the inside of the chicken cavity. Place the thyme, lemon halves, and garlic pieces inside the cavity. Liberally butter the chicken skin and season it with salt and pepper. Place onion quarters around the chicken on all sides. Cover and roast for 1½ to 2 hours or until the chicken is so tender it falls apart. Serve with Garlic Mashed Potatoes* and vegetables.

*See recipe for Garlic Mashed Potatoes

GRILLED CHICKEN KABOBS

Preparation time: 10 minutes
Cook time: 15–20 minutes
Serves: 4

Ingredients:
1 lb. cage-free organic chicken breast, raw
1 recipe Homemade Worcestershire Sauce*
1 organic red bell pepper, sliced
1 organic yellow bell pepper, sliced
Dash of organic sea salt, to taste
Dash of organic black pepper, to taste

Instructions:
Slice the raw chicken into small, bite-sized pieces. In a small bowl, marinade the raw chicken in sauce for at least 2 hours. Soak 4 wooden skewers in water until swollen. Set aside. Slice the peppers into large bite-sized pieces. Evenly divide the peppers and chicken into four equal portions. Using wet skewers, pierce each piece of pepper and chicken in an alternating pattern until each skewer holds one portion. Warm the grill to a medium heat. Grill the kabobs for 15–20 minutes, rotating the skewers often. Serve with chilled Potato Salad.*

*See recipe for Homemade Worcestershire Sauce
*See recipe for Potato Salad

GRILLED CHICKEN KABOBS

GRILLED THYME AND LEMON CHICKEN

Preparation time: 10 minutes
Cook time: 10 minutes
Serves: 4

Ingredients:
1 lb. free-range organic chicken breasts, raw
⅓ cup organic lemon juice
⅓ cup extra virgin olive oil
1 tsp. organic garlic salt
½ tsp. fresh organic thyme leaves

Instructions:
Place the raw chicken in a 9x13 glass pan. In a small bowl, mix the juice, oil, and spices until well combined. Pour the sauce over the chicken, making sure that each piece is covered thoroughly with the marinade. Cover and refrigerate the chicken for at least 6 hours. When ready to cook, warm the grill to a medium heat. Grill the chicken breasts for 10 minutes on each side or until the chicken is thoroughly cooked. Serve with Potato Salad* or a fresh herb salad.

*See recipe for Potato Salad

ITALIAN SAUSAGE AND BACON PIZZA

Preparation time: 30 minutes
Cook time: 20 minutes
Yields: 1 large pizza

Ingredients:
Dough:
3 cups Knight's Nutritious GF Flour Blend
1 tsp. organic clover honey
½ tsp. organic active dry yeast
1⅓ cups ice water
1 Tbsp. extra virgin olive oil
1 tsp. organic sea salt

Toppings:
1 recipe Pizza Sauce*
1 (10 oz.) package dairy and soy-free cheese
½ cup fresh organic oregano
1 (8 oz.) package organic turkey bacon, cooked
¾ cup organic black olives, sliced
½ cup fresh organic onion, chopped
½ cup fresh organic red pepper, chopped
2-3 cups Italian Turkey Sausage*

Seasonings:
Organic Italian seasoning, to taste
Organic garlic powder, to taste
Organic fennel, to taste

Instructions:
Preheat oven to 400 degrees.

Dough:
In small bowl, mix the GF flour, dry yeast and sea salt together until thoroughly combined. While mixing, slowly add the ice water, honey, and oil. Beat on high for 3 minute.

Thoroughly butter and lightly flour a cast iron pizza pan. Drop the dough onto the floured surface of the pan and sprinkle the dough with flour. Gently press the dough to the sides of the pan.

Toppings:
Generously apply pizza sauce to the dough and lightly dust it with Italian seasoning and garlic powder; sprinkle the dough thoroughly with cheese, sausage, and bacon; dust again with Italian Seasoning, garlic and fennel; add the vegetables and oregano; lightly press all the ingredients into the dough. Bake for 20 minutes or until thoroughly cooked.

Hint: Prepare several of these pizzas, cut them in half and freeze them in Food Safe bags for use as frozen pizzas later!

* See recipe for Pizza Sauce
* See recipe for Italian Turkey Sausage

ITALIAN SAUSAGE MEAT PIE

Preparation time: 30 minutes
Cook time: 30-40 minutes
Yields: 1 pie

Ingredients:
1 lb. free-range organic ground beef, browned
1 lb. Italian Turkey Sausage*
½ fresh organic onion, chopped
2 organic celery ribs, chopped
2 tsp. organic minced garlic

Spices:
½ tsp. organic rosemary
½ tsp. organic thyme
¼ tsp. organic marjoram
1 tsp. organic sea salt
¼ tsp. organic black pepper
½ cup water
6 cups hot mashed potatoes (6-8 potatoes)
(Left over potatoes are acceptable)

Instructions:

Preheat oven to 375 degrees.

Prepare 1 Cold Water Pie Crust recipe* that yields two crusts. In a large cast iron skillet, brown the sausage and hamburger. Drain the meat and set it aside. Add a small layer of water to the skillet and sauté the onions, celery, and garlic until soft (1 minute.) Add in the meat and spices and stir thoroughly. Toss in the mashed potatoes and mix well. Place one unbaked pie crust in a 9 inch pie pan. Fill the crust with the meat and potato mixture. Top with the second pie crust. With a fork, gently press the edges of the crust against the lip of the pie pan and trim off the excess. Bake for 30-40 minutes or until the crust is lightly browned. Cool, serve and enjoy!

*See recipe for Italian Turkey Sausage
*See recipe for Cold Water Pie Crust

ITALIAN TURKEY SAUSAGE

Preparation time: 15 minutes
Cook time: 15 minutes
Yields: 1 pound

Ingredients:
1 lb. organic ground turkey, raw
2 Tbsp. organic Italian seasoning
1 Tbsp. organic fennel
1 tsp. organic garlic powder
1½ tsp. organic sea salt
2 tsp. organic oregano
1 tsp. organic paprika
½ tsp. organic onion powder

Instructions:
In a small bowl, combine the raw ground turkey and spices. Mix the spices evenly throughout the raw meat. In a skillet, brown the ground turkey, drain it and set it aside. Use in any recipe that calls for Italian sausage.

Hint: For a stronger sausage flavor, season the cooked sausage with additional spices in a skillet over medium heat.

JUICY BAKED STEAK

Preparation time: 5 minutes
Cook time: 13 minutes
Yields: 1 steak

Ingredients:
1 large organic rib eye steak
1 tsp. extra virgin olive oil
Dash of organic steak seasoning, to taste (or salt and pepper)

Instructions:
Preheat oven to 400 degrees.
Tenderize the steak using a meat mallet. Season to taste with steak seasoning or salt and pepper. Add 1 tsp. of oil to a large cast iron skillet and sear steaks on high for 2 minutes on each side. Next, place the skillet in the preheated oven and bake for 10-13 minutes for a well-done steak. Serve with Potato Salad.*

*See recipe for Potato Salad

MAMA'S MEATLOAF

Preparation time: 10 minutes
Cook time: 1 hour
Serves: 5

Ingredients:
Loaf:
2 lbs. free-range organic ground beef, raw
2 cups organic GF oatmeal
½ cup organic onion, chopped
1 (6 oz.) can organic tomato sauce

Sauce:
1 cup Basic Ketchup*

Instructions:
Preheat oven to 350 degrees.
In a medium sized bowl, combine the raw hamburger, oatmeal, chopped onions, and tomato sauce. Mix until well combined. Pat the hamburger mixture into a 1.5 quart glass pan and cover with ketchup. Bake the meatloaf for 45 minutes to an hour or until it is thoroughly cooked throughout. Serve with Mashed Potatoes* and steamed vegetables.

*See recipe for Basic Ketchup
*See recipe for Mashed Potatoes

MAMA'S MEATLOAF

MUSHROOM AND ONION SCRAMBLE

Preparation time: 10 minutes
Cook time: 5 minutes
Serves: 1

Ingredients:
1 Tbsp. dairy and soy-free butter
2 cage-free organic eggs
¾ cup organic mushrooms, sliced
2 Tbsp. organic green onion, chopped
¼ cup dairy and soy-free cheese, shredded
Dash of organic sea salt, to taste
Dash of organic black pepper, to taste

Instructions:
In a small bowl, whisk the eggs until smooth and set aside. In a frying pan, sauté mushrooms and onions in butter until tender. Add in eggs and cheese. Scramble the entire mixture until it is no longer runny. Remove from heat and season to taste with salt and pepper. Serve with Dad's Fluffy Biscuits.*

*See recipe for Dad's Fluffy Biscuits

POT ROAST

Preparation time: 20 minutes
Cook time: 3-4 hours
Serves: 4

Ingredients:
3 organic potatoes, peeled and quartered
2 large organic carrots, chopped
2 ribs fresh organic celery, chopped
½ cup fresh organic onion, chopped
4 organic bay leaves
2 tsp. organic rosemary
1 tsp. organic thyme
2 tsp. organic sea salt
3-4 cups water (or enough to completely cover the roast)
3-4 lbs. free-range organic beef roast

Instructions:
Combine the roast, water, vegetables, potatoes and seasonings in a large crock pot. Cover and cook for 2-4 hours on high or until the roast is so tender that it falls apart.

ROSEMARY-LEMON CHICKEN

Preparation time: 10 minutes
Cook time: 35 minutes
Serves: 2

Ingredients:
1 lb. free-range organic chicken breast, raw
2 Tbsp. extra virgin olive oil
¼ cup organic lemon juice
2 tsp. organic garlic powder
¼ cup fresh organic rosemary
1 tsp. organic garlic salt

Instructions:
Preheat oven to 350 degrees.
Place the chicken in an 8x8 glass pan. In a small bowl, combine the oil, juice, garlic, rosemary, and salt and mix well. Pour the sauce over the chicken, making sure that the chicken is covered thoroughly. Cover and bake for 30 minutes or until the juice runs clear. Serve with rice and steamed vegetables.

SPINACH SCRAMBLED EGGS

Preparation time: 10 minutes
Cook time: 7 minutes
Serves: 4

Ingredients:
½ cup organic tomatoes, diced
1 cup organic spinach, washed and dried
8 cage-free organic eggs
1 Tbsp. dairy and soy-free butter
1 Tbsp. fresh organic basil, chopped
Dash of organic sea salt, to taste
Dash of organic black pepper, to taste

Instructions:
In a small bowl, whisk the eggs until smooth and set aside. In a frying pan, sauté tomatoes, spinach, and basil in butter until tender. Add the eggs and scramble until no longer runny. Remove from heat and season to taste with salt and pepper. Serve with Dad's Fluffy Biscuits.*

*See recipe for Dad's Fluffy Biscuits

STEAK AND VEGGIE STIR-FRY

Preparation time: 10 minutes
Cook time: 10 minutes
Serves: 2

Ingredients:
1 (8 oz.) package 100% buckwheat soba noodles
¼ cup Alternative Gluten-Free Soy Sauce*
1 Tbsp. organic sesame oil
1 Tbsp. organic minced garlic
1 lb. free-range organic sirloin steak, cut into one inch strips
2 Tbsp. organic rice vinegar
1 tsp. organic ground ginger
3 cups fresh organic broccoli florets
1 organic carrot, shredded

Instructions:
Cook the soba noodles according to package directions, drain and set aside. Fill a sauce pan with water and bring it to a boil. Add the broccoli florets, cover, and blanch for 4 minutes. Drain and set aside. In a frying pan, sauté the carrot and garlic in the soy sauce alternative. Add in the strips of steak and cook to desired doneness (about 10 minutes.) Add the oil, vinegar, and ginger, stirring continually over medium heat. Toss in the broccoli and noodles, stirring occasionally until all the ingredients are well heated. Serve and enjoy!

*See recipe for Alternative Gluten-Free Soy Sauce

STRAWBERRY CHICKEN STIR-FRY

Preparation time: 15 minutes
Cook time: 10 minutes
Serves: 4

Ingredients:
1 organic red bell pepper, sliced lengthwise
1 organic yellow bell pepper, sliced lengthwise
1 organic cucumber, peeled and sliced
1 organic tomato, diced
1 cup organic fresh strawberries, washed and diced
1 lb. cage-free organic chicken, sliced
2 tsp. extra virgin olive oil
⅛ cup organic clover honey
Dash of organic sea salt, to taste
Dash of organic black pepper, to taste
Dash of organic garlic powder, to taste
Pinch of organic basil
Pinch of fresh organic parsley

Instructions:
In a large skillet, fry the chicken breast in a dash of olive oil. When the chicken has cooked completely, set it aside in a separate dish to cool. When cool, cut the chicken breasts into ½ inch strips. Add a dash of oil to the empty frying pan and toss in the vegetables and all the spices except parsley. Sauté the spices and vegetables until they become fragrant. Add in the strips of chicken. Warm the stir-fry over low heat. Top with a drizzle of honey and fresh parsley. Serve over brown rice.

TURKEY BACON OMELET

Preparation time: 10 minutes
Cook time: 5 minutes
Serves: 1

Ingredients:
2 cage-free organic eggs
½ cup organic turkey bacon, cooked
¼ cup fresh organic onion, finely chopped (optional)
¼ cup fresh organic green bell pepper, finely chopped (optional)
¼ cup organic cheddar dairy and soy-free cheese, shredded (optional)
1 Tbsp. dairy and soy free-butter
Dash of organic sea salt, to taste
Dash of organic black pepper, to taste

Instructions:
Chop the vegetables and set aside. Fry the turkey bacon and chop or tear into bite sized pieces. Set aside. In a small bowl, whisk the eggs until smooth and set aside. Add butter to a large skillet and warm over medium heat. When the butter has melted and begun to sizzle, pour in eggs. Evenly sprinkle the chopped vegetables and bacon over one half of the omelet. Distribute the cheese evenly over the bacon and vegetables. Cook until egg is firm enough to turn. Fold the omelet in half, flip and continue to cook until the egg is no longer runny. Cool and serve with buttered Soft and Sweet Honey Bread.*

*See recipe for Soft and Sweet Honey Bread

TURKEY BACON OMELET

TURKEY STUFFED PEPPERS

Preparation time: 15 minutes
Cook time: 30 minutes
Serves: 4

Ingredients:
4 organic yellow, red, or green bell peppers
1 lb. organic ground turkey, browned
1 cup fresh organic cilantro, chopped
¼ cup fresh organic onion, finely chopped
1 tsp. organic basil
1 Tbsp. fresh organic parsley, chopped
2 cups organic chicken stock, reserve 1 cup
1 cup brown rice, cooked

Instructions:
Preheat oven to 350 degrees.
Cut each pepper in half and remove the seeds. Place the peppers cut-side down on a cookie sheet and bake for 15 minutes. Cool. In a large skillet, cook the ground turkey until brown. Drain it and set it aside in a separate bowl. In the skillet, sauté the onions in a dash of water. Finally, add in the spices, rice, stock, and browned turkey. Stir until well combined. Stuff each half pepper with ½ to ¾ cup of the turkey mixture. Drizzle a small amount of the reserved stock over each pepper. Bake the peppers for 15 minutes or until tender. Serve and enjoy!

ZUCCHINI CHICKEN

Preparation time: 20 minutes
Cook time: 3 hours
Serves: 5

Ingredients:
1 tsp. organic sea salt
3 cups organic turkey, cooked and cubed
1 Tbsp. extra virgin olive oil
2 Tbsp. organic minced garlic
1 tsp. organic ground ginger
2 small organic zucchinis, cubed
¼ tsp. organic black pepper
2 tsp. organic dried cilantro
¼ cup fresh organic onion, chopped

Instructions:
In a large crock pot, combine all the ingredients and cook on high for 3-4 hours. Serve with Fantastically Fluffy French Bread.*

*See recipe for Fantastically Fluffy French Bread

DESSERTS & PASTRIES

ASSORTED DESSERTS

DESSERTS & PASTRIES

APPLE CRISP

Preparation time: 20 minutes
Cook time: 35 minutes
Serves: 24

Ingredients:
Crisp:
¾ cup organic GF oatmeal
½ cup organic clover honey
½ cup dairy and soy-free butter
½ cup Knight's Nutritious GF Flour Blend
½ tsp. organic nutmeg
1 tsp. organic cinnamon

Fruit:
3 organic apples, diced

Instructions:
Preheat oven to 350 degrees.
In a small bowl, cream the butter and honey together. Add the dry ingredients and mix together. Set aside. Butter a 9x13 glass pan and place the apples in the bottom. Pour the batter over the apples and spread it evenly to the edges of the pan. Bake the crisp for 35 minutes. Cool and serve.

Hint: Make 2 recipes of crisp for each 3 cups of fruit.

*****Variation 1:** For Peach Crisp: Substitute 3 cups of fresh peaches for apples.

*****Variation 2:** For Pear Crisp: Substitute 3 cups of fresh pears for apples.

BLACK AND WHITE BANANA SQUARES

Preparation time: 10 minutes
Cook time: 25 minutes
Yields: 24

Ingredients:
½ cup dairy and soy-free butter
½ cup organic clover honey
1 cage-free organic egg
1 tsp. pure organic vanilla extract
3-4 organic bananas, mashed
1½ cup Knight's Nutritious GF Flour Blend
1 tsp. organic baking powder
1 tsp. organic baking soda
½ tsp. organic sea salt
¼ cup organic cocoa powder, reserve

Instructions:
Preheat oven to 350 degrees.
In the bowl of a stand mixer, cream together the butter, honey, and vanilla. In a small bowl, mash the bananas and mix them with the eggs. Add the banana mixture to the butter mixture and blend well. In a separate bowl, combine the flour, baking powder, soda and salt. Mix well. Add the dry ingredient to wet ingredients and mix on high for 3-4 minutes to add air to batter. Once well mixed, divide the batter into two equal parts and add a ¼ cup of cocoa powder to one portion. In a well-buttered pan, spread the cocoa batter evenly across the bottom of the pan. Spoon the remaining white batter on top of the cocoa batter and spread it evenly to the edges. Bake for 25 minutes. Cool, serve and enjoy!

CINNAMON ROLLS

Preparation time: 30 minutes
Cook time: 30 minutes
Yields: 12-14

Ingredients:
Dough:
3½ cups Knight's Nutritious GF Flour Blend
2½ Tbsp. organic clover honey
1 tsp. organic sea salt
4½ tsp. organic active dry yeast
1 cup organic rice milk, unsweetened, lukewarm
¼ cup dairy and soy free-butter
1 cage-free organic egg

Filling:
1 recipe Date Glaze Variation 1*
½ cup dairy and soy-free butter, room temperature, reserve

Instructions:
Preheat oven to 350 degrees

Filling:
Prepare 1 recipe of Date Glaze* according to the directions. The mixture will be very thick, but spreadable. Add more milk if it is not loose enough. Add additional cinnamon until the filling has an extremely potent cinnamon flavor.

Dough:

While the dates are softening for the filling, begin to prepare the cinnamon roll dough. Warm the honey and butter until both are melted; stir and set aside. Combine the flour, salt, and yeast in the bowl of a stand mixer. Slowly beat the warm rice milk into the flour mixture to form small crumbly balls. Add in the butter and honey mixture. Mix until completely blended. Toss in the egg while continuing to beat the mixture on a low speed. When all the ingredients have been added, beat on high for 2-3 minutes to add air to dough. Generously flour the surface of a pastry mat and rolling pin. Lightly dust the dough with flour and gently scrape it from bowl onto the mat. The dough will be very delicate and fluffy. Roll out the dough until it is approximately an ⅛ inch thick. Generously spread the reserved butter on the surface of the dough. Sprinkle it with a liberal layer of cinnamon and let it stand for 2 minutes.

Roll:

Spread the warm date filling evenly over the well-buttered dough. Carefully form the dough into one long cinnamon roll. Gently pull the roll to lengthen it, allowing for more cinnamon rolls. Using a 12-inch piece of thread, cut the roll into 2 inch slices. Place the slices onto a cast iron pan and allow the rolls to touch each other. Cover the rolls with a piece of wax paper or buttered parchment paper. Let them rise for 1 hour or until they have doubled in size. Bake for 20-25 minutes or until the tops are lightly brown. Top with Vanilla Butter Glaze* and enjoy!

*See recipe for Date Glaze Variation 1
*See recipe for Vanilla Butter Glaze

CINNAMON ROLLS

COCONUT VANILLA ICE CREAM

Preparation time: 30 minutes
Chill time: 2 hours
Yields: 1 quart

Ingredients:
2 (15. oz.) cans organic, full-fat coconut milk, unsweetened
¼ cup organic agave nectar
1 tsp. pure organic vanilla extract
2 organic vanilla bean, seeds
½ cup organic clover honey

Instructions:
In the bowl of a stand mixer, combine the milk, honey, agave nectar, extract, and bean seeds. Blend until smooth. Pour the milk mixture into an ice cream maker and mix for 60 minutes or until desired consistency is achieved. Chill overnight. Serve and enjoy!

Hint: To prepare a vanilla bean, cut off the top of the bean, cut the bean in half, and the remove seeds. Add the seeds to the recipe.

Variation 1: For Peanut Butter Cup Vanilla Ice Cream: Make one recipe of Dark Chocolate Peanut Butter Cups. One minute before the ice cream is ready to be removed from the ice cream maker, chop the frozen peanut butter cups into bite sized chunks. In a freezer-safe container, alternate layers of prepared ice cream with layers of peanut butter chunks. Freeze overnight. Serve and enjoy!

*Variation 2: For Strawberry Ice Cream: Preheat oven to 400 degrees. Line a cookie sheet with parchment paper and spread 2 cups of fresh, organic strawberries (washed, stemmed and diced) evenly onto the pan. Roast the strawberries for 20 minutes. Turn them after the first 10 minutes. Cool. When the ice cream is ready, alternate layers of ice cream with layers of strawberries in a freeze-safe container. Freeze overnight. Serve and enjoy!

*See recipe for Dark Chocolate Peanut Butter Cups

PEANUT BUTTER CUP VANILLA ICE CREAM

COLD WATER PIE CRUST

Preparation time: 10 minutes
Cook time: 0 minutes
Yields: 2 pie crusts or one crust and one top

Ingredients:
2 cup Knight's Nutritious GF Flour Blend
½ tsp. organic sea salt
⅔ cup dairy and soy-free butter
4-6 Tbsp. ice water

Instructions:
In a small bowl, mix the flour and salt together. Using a pastry cutter, cut in the butter. Add in 1 Tbsp. of cold water at a time until the dough becomes pliable but not sticky. Divide the dough into equal halves. Lightly flour a pastry mat and a rolling pin. Roll one portion of the dough to desired thickness and place it in a 9 inch pie pan. (If the consistency of the dough is not conducive to rolling, place the dough in the pie pan and spread it to the edges using your hands.) Fill the crust with filling. On a well-floured pastry mat, spread the second portion of dough to desired thickness. For a lattice top, cut ½ inch strips of dough and cover the pie filling with strips in a lattice design. For a complete top, carefully transfer the layer of rolled dough to the top of the pie. Using a fork, firmly press the edges of the dough onto the lip of the pie pan and trim off the excess.

Hint: For pudding pies, bake the crust in a 350 degree oven for 8 minutes and cool before adding the filling.

DARK CHOCOLATE CAKE

Preparation time: 10 minutes
Cook time: 35 minutes
Serves: 4

Ingredients:
2 cups Knight's Nutritious GF Flour Blend
¼ cup organic cocoa powder, unsweetened
¼ tsp. organic sea salt
½ tsp. organic baking soda
1 cup organic agave nectar
2 cage-free organic eggs
1 Tbsp. pure organic vanilla extract
⅓ cup extra virgin olive oil
¼ cup of water

Frost with Chocolate Icing*
Garnish with ½ cup organic walnuts, chopped, (optional)
3 fresh organic raspberries, (optional)

Instructions:

Preheat oven to 350 degrees.

For a single layer cake, butter a 9 inch cake pan and lightly dust it with flour. For a double layer cake, butter two 4 inch cake pans and lightly dust them with flour.

In a separate bowl, mix the agave nectar and vanilla together. Set aside. In the bowl of a stand mixer, combine the flour, cocoa powder, salt, and soda. Mix until well combined. Slowly add the water and oil to the dry ingredients. Add in the agave mixture and mix well. While continuing to mix, add in one egg. Wait until the first egg has been completely mixed in before adding the second egg. When all the ingredients have been added, beat the batter on high for 3-4 minutes to add air to it. Separate the batter into two equal portions and pour each into a buttered cake pan. Bake the cakes for 30-35 minutes or until they are thoroughly cooked. Cool, remove from pans and frost the first cake with a generous layer of Chocolate Icing.* Place the second layer cake on top of the iced cake and liberally frost the entire cake. Decorate it with nuts and fresh raspberries. Serve with homemade Coconut Vanilla Ice Cream.*

*See recipe for Vanilla Icing Variation 1
*See recipe for Coconut Vanilla Ice Cream

DARK CHOCOLATE PEANUT BUTTER CUPS

Preparation time: 15 minutes
Chill time: 1 hour
Serves: 12

Ingredients:
Peanut butter filling:
1 Tbsp. organic coconut oil, melted
1 Tbsp. pure organic maple syrup
1 tsp. pure organic vanilla extract
¾ cup organic creamy peanut butter

Chocolate top and bottom layers:
3 tsp. organic cocoa powder, unsweetened
1 tsp. pure organic vanilla extract
1½ Tbsp. pure organic maple syrup
¼ cup organic coconut oil, melted

Instructions:
Place paper liners in a 12 cup pan and set aside.

Bottom:
Combine 1 chocolate layer recipe in the order listed and mix until creamy. If needed, warm the entire mixture over low heat to maintain a liquid consistency. Spread 1 to 1½ teaspoons of chocolate in the bottom of each cup and freeze on a level surface for 10 minutes.

Filling:
While the bottom chocolate layers are freezing, mix the peanut butter filling recipe in order listed and blend until creamy. (For a less dense peanut butter texture, reduce the peanut butter by an ⅛ of a cup. Do not increase coconut oil. It will cause the mixture to be too oily.) Spoon 2 teaspoons of filling onto each frozen chocolate layer and smooth to the edge of the cups. Freeze for another 15 minutes on a level surface.

Top:
While the middle layers are freezing, mix 2 chocolate layer recipes in the order listed and blend until creamy. Cover each peanut butter layer with 2-3 Tbsp. of chocolate or until peanut butter is completely covered. Finally, freeze for 30 minutes on a level surface. Remove from freezer and serve immediately, or chop into pieces and mix into homemade Coconut Vanilla Ice Cream.*

*See recipe for Coconut Vanilla Ice Cream

DARK CHOCOLATE PEANUT BUTTER CUPS

DATE GLAZE

Preparation time: 20 minutes
Cook time: 10 minutes
Yields: 1½ cups

Ingredients:
8-10 organic dates
⅓-½ cup organic coconut oil, unsweetened
½-1 cup organic coconut milk, room temperature
¼-⅓ cup organic agave nectar
2-3 tsp. pure organic vanilla extract

Instructions:
In a small skillet, combine the dates and coconut oil over low heat and melt for about 30 minutes. As the dates soften, mash them and remove the pits. When the consistency of the dates becomes very mushy, slowly add the room temperature coconut milk and stir until the mixture becomes loose enough to spread. Mix in the agave nectar and vanilla. Stir over low heat until well combined. If the consistency is not loose enough, add more milk and agave. For best results, use while warm.

*Variation 1: For Chocolate Glaze: Add a ½-1 cup of organic cocoa powder and a dash of organic, unsweetened coconut milk to loosen the consistency.

*Variation 2: For Cinnamon Glaze: Add a ¼-½ cup of organic cinnamon (more if needed.)

*Variation 3: For Lemon Glaze: Add a ¼ cup of organic lemon juice and a dash of organic lemon zest to taste.

*Variation 4: For Maple Glaze: Add 1-2 Tbsp. of organic maple extract and a dash of pure organic maple syrup to taste.

HOMEMADE APPLE PIE

Preparation time: 30 minutes
Cook time: 35–40 minutes
Yields: 1 pie

Ingredients:
Crust:
1 recipe Cold Water Pie Crust*

Filling:
⅓ cup organic clover honey, melted
¼ cup Knight's Nutritious GF Flour Blend
1 tsp. organic cinnamon
1 tsp. organic nutmeg
8 organic apples, peeled and sliced
2 Tbsp. diary and soy-free butter, melted
Dash of organic sea salt

Instructions:
Preheat oven to 425 degrees.
Crust: Prepare one recipe of Cold Water Pie Crust* and reserve half of the dough.

Filling: In a small bowl, combine the flour, cinnamon, nutmeg, and salt. Set aside. Place the apples in a large bowl. Cover them with melted honey and butter. Toss until all the apples are coated. Pour the flour mixture over the sweetened apples and toss to coat. Transfer the filling into the pie crust. Top with one recipe of Sweet Strudel Topping.* For a lattice top, cut the dough into ½ inch strips and cover filling with pastry strips in a lattice design.

*See recipe for Cold Water Pie Crust
*See recipe for Sweet Strudel Topping

LEMON BARS

Preparation time: 20 minutes
Cook time: 20 minutes
Yields: 24 bars

Ingredients:
Lemon Filling:
3 cage-free organic eggs and 2 egg yolks
6 Tbsp. pure organic maple syrup
⅓ cup organic lemon juice
1 Tbsp. organic lemon zest
⅓ cup Knight's Nutritious GF Flour Blend

Crust:
1 cup Knight's Nutritious GF Flour Blend
⅛ cup organic clover honey
⅛ cup pure organic maple syrup
½ cup dairy and soy-free butter

Instructions:
Preheat oven to 350 degrees.
Crust:
Line an 8x8 glass pan with parchment paper and set aside. Combine the wet ingredients and blend until smooth. Add in the flour and mix thoroughly. Pour the crust into the pan and bake for 10-15 minutes or until it is golden brown.

Filling:
In the bowl of a stand mixer, combine the eggs and yolks. Beat until foamy. Add in the syrup, juice, zest, and flour. Mix all the ingredients until thoroughly blended. Pour the mixture over the cooling crust and bake it until the center sets up (about 20 minutes.) Cool and serve.

MOLASSES CAKE COOKIES

Preparation time: 10 minutes
Cook time: 9-10 minutes
Yields: 24

Ingredients:
½ tsp. pure organic vanilla extract
¾ cup unsulphured black strap molasses
¾ cup organic coconut oil, room temperature
¼ cup pure organic maple syrup
2 cage-free organic eggs
1 tsp. organic cinnamon
½ tsp. organic ground cloves
1 tsp. organic baking soda
2½ cup Knight's Nutritious GF Flour Blend

Instructions:
In a small bowl, combine the cinnamon, cloves, soda, and flour. Set aside. In the bowl of a stand mixer, cream the vanilla, molasses, oil, syrup, and eggs until silky. While continuing to mix, fold the dry ingredients into the wet ingredients. The dough will be sticky. Refrigerate the batter for at least on hour. When ready to bake, preheat the oven to 350 degrees. Dust your hands with flour, roll the chilled dough into ½ inch balls and place them evenly on a baking sheet. Flatten each cookie slightly with your palm. Sprinkle the top of each cookie with a pinch of cinnamon and bake for 9-10 minutes. Cool and serve.

OATMEAL COOKIES

Preparation time: 15 minutes
Cook time: 10 minutes
Serves: 24

Ingredients:
1 cup dairy and soy-free butter, softened
½ cup organic clover honey
¼ cup unsulphured black strap molasses
¼ cup pure organic maple syrup
2 cage-free organic eggs
1 tsp. pure organic vanilla extract
½ tsp. organic sea salt
3½ cup Knight's Nutritious GF Flour Blend
1 tsp. organic baking soda
3 cups organic GF oats

Instructions:
Preheat oven to 350 degrees.
In the bowl of a stand mixer, cream the butter, honey, molasses, and syrup until smooth. Mix in the eggs and vanilla. In a separate bowl, combine the flour, salt, soda, and oats and add it to the wet ingredients. Beat the dough on high for 2 minutes. It will be very sticky. Refrigerate it for 20 minutes. Remove the batter from refrigerator and roll it into 1 inch balls. Place the balls evenly on a baking sheet and flatten them slightly with your palm. Bake for 10 minutes. Cool on a cooling rake. Serve and enjoy!

***Variation 1:** For Oatmeal-Apple Cookies: Add 2 peeled and diced organic apples and ½ to 1 tsp. of organic cinnamon.

***Variation 2:** For Oatmeal-Raisin Cookies: Add 1 cup of organic, unsweetened raisins.

PEANUT BUTTER COOKIES

Preparation time: 10 minutes
Cook time: 7-8 minutes
Yields: 2 dozen

Ingredients:
2½ Tbsp. organic clover honey
1 Tbsp. unsulphured black strap molasses
1½ Tbsp. pure organic maple syrup
½ cup dairy and soy-free butter
1 cup organic creamy peanut butter
1 cage-free organic egg
1½ cup Knight's Nutritious GF Flour Blend
1 tsp. organic baking soda
2 Tbsp. rice or coconut milk, unsweetened
1 tsp. pure organic vanilla extract

Instructions:
Preheat oven to 375 degrees.
In the bowl of a stand mixer, blend the honey, molasses, syrup, and butter on a medium speed. Add in the peanut butter, egg, milk, and vanilla and blend until smooth. Finally, add in the flour and baking soda and beat on high for 1 minute. If the dough is too soft to roll into balls, refrigerate it for 20 minutes or until firm. Form the dough into 1 inch balls and place them evenly on a cookie sheet. Using a moistened fork, imprint each cookie with a crossed fork pattern. Bake for 7-8 minutes. Cool on a cooling rack. Serve and enjoy!

PEANUT BUTTER TEFF COOKIES

Preparation time: 10 minutes
Cook time: 11 minutes
Yields: 24

Ingredients:
1 cup + 1 Tbsp. organic peanut butter
2 tsp. pure organic vanilla extract
½ cup extra virgin olive oil
½ cup pure organic maple syrup
½ tsp. organic sea salt
¼ tsp. organic xanthan gum
1 ½ cup organic teff flour

Instructions:
Preheat oven to 350 degrees.
In the bowl of a stand mixer, combine the peanut butter, vanilla, oil, and syrup. Beat until creamy. In a separate bowl, combine the salt, xanthan gum, and teff flour. Slowly add the dry ingredients to the wet ingredients while mixing on a low medium speed. Refrigerate the dough for 10 minutes. Form the chilled dough into 1 inch balls and place them evenly on a cookie sheet. Using a moistened fork, imprint each cookie with a crossed fork pattern. Bake for 11 minutes. Cool and serve.

PUMPKIN BARS

Preparation time: 20 minutes
Cook time: 30 minutes
Yields: 24

Ingredients:
Bars:
¾ cup dairy and soy-free butter
1 cup organic clover honey
2 (16 oz.) cans organic pumpkin
4 cage-free organic eggs
2 cups Knight's Nutritious GF Flour Blend
2 tsp. organic baking powder
1½ tsp. organic cinnamon
½ tsp. organic baking soda
½ tsp. organic sea salt
½ tsp. organic nutmeg

Frosting:
1 recipe Vanilla Icing*

Instructions:
Preheat oven to 350 degrees.
In the bowl of a stand mixer, cream the butter, honey, pumpkin, and eggs. Beat until well combined. In a separate bowl, mix together the flour, soda, powder, salt, cinnamon, and nutmeg. Add the dry ingredients to the wet ingredients and beat for 2 minutes. Butter a jelly roll pan and spread the pumpkin mixture evenly in the pan. Bake for 30 minutes. Cool and frost with Vanilla Icing.* Serve and enjoy!

*See recipe for Vanilla Icing

PUMPKIN COOKIES

Preparation time: 15 minutes
Cook time: 10 minutes
Serves: 24

Ingredients:
1½ cups Knight's Nutritious GF Flour Blend
2 tsp. organic baking powder
½ tsp. organic baking soda
½ tsp. organic sea salt
1 tsp. organic cinnamon
½ tsp. organic nutmeg
⅔ cup dairy and soy-free butter, softened
¼ cup organic clover honey
¼ cup unsulphured black strap molasses
¼ pure organic maple syrup
2 cage-free organic eggs, beaten
1¼ cup organic pumpkin
1 tsp. pure organic vanilla extract
1 cup organic GF oats
1 cup chopped organic dates (optional)
½ cup chopped organic pecans (optional)
Dash of organic ground cloves

Instructions:
In the bowl of a stand mixer, cream the butter, honey, molasses, and syrup. Add the pumpkin, vanilla, and eggs. Blend for 1 minute. Slowly add in the dry ingredient and beat until smooth. Refrigerate the batter for 20 minutes. When ready to bake, preheat the oven to 350 degrees. Form the chilled dough into quarter sized balls. Place them on a baking sheet and flatten them slightly with your palm. Bake for 10 minutes. Cool on a cooling rack. Serve and enjoy.

SNICKER DOODLE DANDIES

Preparation time: 10 minutes
Cook time: 10 minutes
Yields: 24

Ingredients:
2¼ cup Knight's Nutritious GF Flour Blend
1 tsp. organic baking powder
½ tsp. organic xanthan gum
1 cage-free organic egg
½ cup organic clover honey
½ cup organic coconut oil, melted
2 tsp. pure organic vanilla extract
2 Tbsp. organic cinnamon

Instructions:
Preheat oven to 350 degrees.
In the bowl of a stand mixer, combine the egg, honey, oil, and vanilla. Mix until well combined. In a separate bowl, combine the flour, baking powder, and gum. Add the dry ingredients to the wet ingredients and mix well. Refrigerate the dough for 1 hour. Wet hands and roll the chilled dough into 1 inch size balls. Place the balls on a baking sheet and flatten slightly with your palm. Dab each cookie with a little water and lightly sprinkle them with cinnamon. Bake for 10 minutes. Cool on a cooling rack. Serve and enjoy!

STRAWBERRY-RHUBARB OATMEAL BARS

Preparation time: 20 minutes
Cook time: 25–30 minutes
Yields: 12

Ingredients:
Fruit Filling
2 Tbsp. organic corn starch
2 Tbsp. warm water
1 cup fresh organic strawberries, stemmed, washed, and chopped
1 cup fresh organic rhubarb, washed and chopped
¼ cup pure organic maple syrup
½ tsp. pure organic vanilla extract

Crust/Topping:
2½ cup organic GF oats
1 tsp. organic cinnamon
⅛ tsp. organic nutmeg
¼ tsp. pure organic vanilla extract
1 cup organic almond butter
¼ cup pure organic maple syrup
¼ cup organic clover honey
¼ cup Rich Apple Butter*
1 cage-free organic egg, beaten

Instructions:
Preheat oven to 325 degrees.
Line an 8x8 glass pan with parchment paper and set aside.

Filling:
In a small bowl, completely dissolve the corn starch in water. Set aside. In a sauce pan, combine the strawberries, rhubarb, vanilla, and syrup. Bring the mixture to a slow boil. Stir it until the rhubarb and strawberries are completely covered in syrup. Remove the pan from heat and add in the corn starch mixture, stirring continually until the liquid is smooth. Set aside to thicken.

Crust/Topping:
In the bowl of stand mixer, combine all the ingredients except the oats. Mix well. Add in the oats and mix until the oats are completely coated with the syrup mixture. Reserve ¾ cup of the batter. Pour the remaining oat mixture in the pan lined with parchment paper. Press the crust to the edges of the pan. Pour the filling over the crust and sprinkle it with the reserved topping. Lightly press the oat topping into the filling. Bake for 25-30 minutes or until the top is lightly brown. Cool, cut, and serve.

*See recipe for Rich Apple Butter

SWEET STRUDEL TOPPING

Preparation time: 5 minutes
Cook time: 0 minutes
Yields: 1½ cups

Ingredients:
½ cup organic clover honey
1 Tbsp. unsulphured black strap molasses
1 cup Knight's Nutritious GF Flour Blend (more if needed)
½ tsp. organic nutmeg
1 tsp. organic cinnamon

Instructions:
In a small bowl, combine all the ingredients except the flour and stir until smooth. Add in the flour and mix until a crumbly texture is achieved. Use this topping as a substitute in any recipe that calls for strudel.

VANILLA ICING

Preparation time: 10 minutes
Chill time: 30 minutes
Yields: 2 cups

Ingredients:
½ Tbsp. organic agave nectar
1 Tbsp. pure organic vanilla extract
1 cup organic palm shorting
½ cup organic clover honey
3-4 Tbsp. organic coconut oil, melted
4 Tbsp. organic tapioca starch
4 Tbsp. Knight's Nutritious GF Flour Blend
¼ tsp. organic sea salt
½ vanilla bean seeds (optional)

Instructions:
Using a hand mixer, blend the nectar, vanilla (bean), shortening, and honey in a small bowl. Add in the starch, flour, and salt. Mix until smooth. While blending, slowly pour in the coconut oil. Chill for 30 minutes. Stir vigorously and frost as desired.

*Variation 1: Chocolate Icing: Add ¼ cup of organic cocoa powder and a dash of organic, unsweetened coconut milk to loosen the consistency.

*Variation 2: Lemon Icing: Add 1-2 tsp. of pure organic lemon extract and 1 Tbsp. of organic lemon juice.

*Variations 3: Maple Icing: Add 1-2 tsp. of pure organic maple extract and substitute 1 Tbsp. of pure organic maple syrup for the agave nectar.

**Vanilla Butter Glaze:
To make a glaze instead of an icing, substitute 1 cup of dairy and soy-free butter for shortening. The consistency will be very loose. For best results, glaze desserts while they are still warm.

*Variation 1: For Chocolate Butter Glaze: Add ¼ cup of organic cocoa powder and a dash of organic, unsweetened coconut milk to loosen the consistency.

*Variation 2: For Lemon Butter Glaze: Add 1-2 tsp. of pure organic lemon extract and 1 Tbsp. of organic lemon juice.

*Variation 3: For Maple Butter Glaze: Add 1-2 tsp. of pure organic maple extract and substitute 1 Tbsp. of pure organic maple syrup for the agave nectar.

Breads, Biscuits & Muffins

ASSORTED BREADS

BREADS, BISCUITS & MUFFINS

APPLE-CINNAMON DELIGHTS

Preparation time: 10 minutes
Cook time: 15 minutes
Yields: 24

Ingredients:
¾ cup organic quinoa, cooked
1 cup organic GF oats, uncooked
1½ tsp. organic cinnamon
½ tsp. organic nutmeg
2 tsp. pure organic maple syrup
1 tsp. unsulphured black strap molasses
½ Tbsp. organic clover honey
1 Tbsp. organic agave nectar
1 organic apple, chopped
2 cage-free organic eggs, beaten

Instructions:
Preheat oven to 350 degrees.
Generously butter a 24 cup mini muffin pan and set it aside. In a medium sized bowl, combine the cinnamon, nutmeg, syrup, molasses, honey, and agave and mix well. Add in the oats and quinoa and stir to coat with the syrup mixture. Finally, add in the eggs and apples and lightly mix. Fill each cup approximately ¾ full and bake for 15 minutes. Cool and serve.

BEST BANANA BREAD

Preparation time: 15 minutes
Cook time: 60 minutes
Yields: 2 loaves

Ingredients:
1 cup extra virgin olive oil
1 cup organic clover honey
4 cage-free organic eggs
4 organic bananas, mashed
¼ cup organic rice milk
2 tsp. organic baking soda
½ tsp. organic sea salt
4 cups Knight's Nutritious GF Flour Blend

Instructions:
Preheat oven to 350 degrees.
Butter two cast iron or glass loaf pans and set them aside. In a separate bowl, mash the bananas until they are very smooth. Set aside. In the bowl of a stand mixer, mix the flour, salt and soda until well combined. While mixing, add the milk and honey to the dry ingredients and mix until a crumbly consistency is achieved. Toss in the bananas and mix thoroughly. Add in the eggs one at a time. Allow each egg to be completely mixed before adding the next. After all ingredients have been added, beat the batter on high for 3-4 minutes to add air to it. Separate the dough into two even portions and pour each half into one pan. Using a wet spatula, carefully smooth the batter to the sides of the pan. Bake for 60 minutes or until thoroughly cooked. Cool and serve with warm dairy and soy-free butter.

BODACIOUS BROWN BREAD

Preparation time: 15 minutes
Cook time: 30 minutes
Yields: 1 loaf

Ingredients:
2¼ tsp. organic active dry yeast
1 cup warm water
¾ cup organic buckwheat flour
3 cups Knight's Nutritious GF Flour Blend
1 tsp. organic sea salt
4 tsp. organic coconut milk, unsweetened
1 Tbsp. extra virgin olive oil
2 cage-free organic eggs
2 Tbsp. unsulphured black strap molasses
2 Tbsp. organic agave nectar
1 tsp. pure organic vanilla extract
½ tsp. organic xanthan gum

Instructions:
Butter and flour a bread pan and set aside.

In the bowl of a stand mixer, combine the flour, gum, salt, and yeast. Mix thoroughly. Next, slowly pour the warm water and milk into the dry ingredients and mix until the dough forms small balls. Add in the agave, molasses, and vanilla. Mix until thoroughly combined. Pour in the oil and mix for 1 minute. Finally, add in the eggs one at a time. When all the ingredients have been added, beat the dough on high for 3 minutes to add air to it. Pour the dough into the prepared pan. Using a wet spatula, very gently move the dough to the corners of the pan. Sprinkle the dough lightly with water and carefully smooth the surface. Cover it with a piece of buttered parchment paper and set it in a warm place. Allow the loaf to rise for 1 hour. When ready to bake, preheat the oven to 350 degrees. Cook for 30 minutes or until done. Cool, remove from the pan and serve it with organic peanut butter and organic clover honey.

CINNAMON TOAST MUFFINS

Preparation time: 15 minutes
Cook time: 25 minutes
Yields: 12

Ingredients:
Bread:
3 cups Fantastically Fluffy French Bread,* diced
¾-1 cup coconut milk, unsweetened
2 cage-free organic eggs
1½ Tbsp. organic clover honey
1 tsp. pure organic vanilla extract
Dash of organic cinnamon

Cinnamon Strudel:
¼ cup dairy and soy-free butter, cold
⅛ cup pure organic maple syrup
⅛ cup unsulphured black strap molasses
¼-¾ cup Knight's Nutritious GF Flour Blend
⅛ tsp. organic cinnamon
Dash of organic sea salt
(Reserve an additional ½ cup of diary and soy-free butter)
(Reserve an additional ½ cup of GF flour)

Instructions:
Muffins:

In a small bowl, mix the milk, eggs, honey, vanilla, and cinnamon until well combined. Set aside. Butter or line a 12 cup muffin pan with paper cups. Add a ½ cup of bread to each cup (more if needed.) Pour the wet mixture evenly over each muffin. Cover and refrigerate for 3 hours.

Strudel:

In a small bowl combine the butter, syrup, molasses, flour, cinnamon, and salt until a crumbly texture is achieved. Melt and mix ¼-½ cup of the reserved butter with strudel to add moisture.

Preheat oven to 350 degrees.

When ready to bake, sprinkle each muffin with strudel. Lightly press the strudel into the wet bread to keep it from falling off during baking. Bake the muffins for 13-15 minutes. (Do not over-bake or the muffins will be dry.) Cool and serve with warm butter, maple syrup and fresh fruit.

DAD'S FLUFFY BISCUITS

Preparation time: 15 minutes
Cook time: 15 minutes
Serves: 12

Ingredients:
4 cups Knight's Nutritious GF Flour Blend
2 Tbsp. organic baking powder
½ cup extra virgin olive oil
1½ cups organic rice milk, unsweetened

Instructions:
Preheat the oven to 425 degrees.
In a large bowl, combine the flour and baking powder and mix to combine. Add in the oil and milk. Mix gently until the dough is very sticky.

To shape the biscuits, wet hands and form a palm sized ball. Drop the dough onto a baking sheet, lightly wet the top of each ball and gently smooth the surface of each biscuit. Bake for 15 minutes or until the biscuits are golden brown. Serve with warm dairy and soy-free butter and organic clover honey.

DELICIOUS DINNER ROLLS

Preparation time: 15 minutes
Cook time: 10 minutes
Yields: 6 rolls

Ingredients:
1½ cup Knight's Nutritious GF Flour Blend
1 tsp. organic active dry yeast
1 Tbsp. organic clover honey
½ tsp. organic sea salt
2 Tbsp. organic dairy and soy-free butter, melted
1 cage-free organic egg
½ cup organic apple juice (1 apple)
½ tsp. pure organic vanilla extract

Wash
1 egg yolk
1 Tbsp. butter
Dash of water

Instructions:
In the bowl of a stand mixer, combine flour, yeast, and salt. While mixing, add in the apple juice to achieve a crumbly texture. In a separate bowl, melt together the honey and butter. Let cool. Add the vanilla to the honey mixture and stir well. Add the honey mixture and egg to the dry ingredients. Beat the dough on high for 3-4 minutes to add air to it. The texture will be very tender and sticky. Using a well-buttered spatula, transfer dough to a buttered bowl and cover with a piece of buttered parchment paper. Allow to rise for 1½-2 hours or until double in size. Cover bowl with a lid and refrigerate overnight.

Preheat oven to 350 degrees.
Butter a baking sheet and lightly dust with flour. Set aside.

Generously flour a pastry mat and turn the dough onto the floured surface. (*Always work very delicately with gluten-free dough.*) Divide the dough into six even portions. Lightly dust each portion with flour and press them each into a square shape. Gather the opposite edges together until all the sides meet in the middle. Lightly pinch the edges together. Carefully turn the rolls over and place the gathered side down on the mat. Gently press the top of the dough with a cupped hand to shape it. Using both hands, shape each roll by shifting it in a circle between well-floured hands along the surface of the mat. When all the rolls have been shaped, carefully slide each one onto the buttered baking sheet. (Be careful not to distort the shape during the transfer.) Cover the finished rolls with a piece of buttered parchment paper. Allow them to rise in a warm place for 45 minutes. Once the dough has risen, remove the paper and cover each roll with a little egg wash. Bake for 18-20 minutes, being careful not to over-cook. Serve as dinner rolls or hamburger buns.

FANTASTICALLY FLUFFY FRENCH BREAD

Preparation time: 20 minutes
Cook time: 25-30 minutes
Yields: 1 loaf

Ingredients:
1½ cup Knight's Nutritious GF Flour Blend
1½ tsp. organic xanthan gum
1 tsp. organic sea salt
1 Tbsp. organic active dry yeast
1 cage-free organic egg
1 Tbsp. organic clover honey
¾ cup organic rice milk, unsweetened, lukewarm
1 Tbsp. dairy and soy-free butter, melted
2 egg whites, lightly beaten
½ tsp. organic apple cider vinegar
Melted butter and 1 egg yolk (optional topping)

Instructions:
Butter one bread pan and set it aside.
In the bowl of a stand mixer, combine the flour, gum, salt, and yeast and mix thoroughly. In a separate bowl, melt the honey and butter together. Add the vinegar to the butter mixture, stir, and set it aside. While mixing the dry ingredients, slowly pour in the milk and allow the dough to form small balls. Add in the butter mixture and mix until thoroughly combined. Finally, toss in the egg and egg whites and beat on high for 3 minutes to add air to the dough. Transfer the dough to the bread pan and let it rise for 60-90 minutes. When ready to bake, preheat the oven to 350 degrees. Bake for 25-30 minutes. Let it cool until the bread sweats in the pan. Remove the bread from the pan and continue to cool. Serve with warm butter and enjoy!

GARLIC FRENCH BREAD

Preparation time: 1 hour
Cook time: 30 minutes
Yields: 1 loaf

Ingredients:
1-2 cups dairy and soy-free butter, melted (more if needed)
4-6 Tbsp. organic garlic powder (more if needed)
2 Tbsp. organic parsley
1 recipe Fantastically Fluffy French Bread*

Instructions:
Prepare and bake 1 recipe of Fantastically Fluffy French Bread. When the bread has thoroughly cooled, slice it into desired sizes and generously butter one side of each piece and place on a baking sheet. Liberally sprinkle the buttered sides with garlic powder and garnish with a dash of parsley. Broil the garlic bread for 1-2 minutes or until the tops are golden brown. Cool, serve and enjoy!

*See recipe for Fantastically Fluffy French Bread

GOLDEN CORN BREAD

Preparation time: 15 minutes
Cook time: 20-25 minutes
Yields: 1 loaf

Ingredients:
1 cup organic yellow corn meal
1 cup Knight's Nutritious GF Flour Blend
2 Tbsp. organic clover honey
4 tsp. organic baking powder
½ tsp. organic sea salt
1 cup organic rice milk, unsweetened
1 cage-free organic egg
¼ cup extra virgin olive oil

Instructions:
Preheat oven to 425 degrees.
In the bowl of a stand mixer, combine the corn meal, flour, baking powder and salt. Mix for 2 minutes. Next, while continuing to mix, add in the milk, egg, oil and honey. Beat for 3 minutes or until smooth. Butter and lightly flour a cast iron or glass bread pan and pour in the batter. Bake for 20-25 minutes or until the top is golden brown. Cool and serve with Chunky Chili.*

GRANOLA BREAKFAST CEREAL

Preparation time: 15 minutes
Cook time: 45 minutes
Yields: 4 cups

Ingredients:
3 cups assorted organic nuts
1 cup organic pumpkin seeds
1 cup organic raisins
½ tsp. organic cinnamon
1 Tbsp. pure organic vanilla extract
Dash of organic sea salt
1 Tbsp. organic clover honey (optional topping)
¼ cup dried fruit (optional topping)

Instructions:
Place the nuts and seeds in a medium sized bowl, cover with water and soak overnight. Soak the raisins separately in 1 cup of water.

The following day, preheat the oven to 250 degrees. Puree the soft raisin and water mixture. Set aside. Drain and rinse the nuts and seeds. Mix the nuts and seeds into the raisin puree. In a food processor, blend the entire mixture until finely chopped. Add in the vanilla, cinnamon, and salt. Stir until well combined. Spread on a small baking sheet and cook for 45 minutes. Cool and drizzle with organic honey and sprinkle with dried fruit. Serve and enjoy!

HERB BREAD

Preparation time: 30 minutes
Cook time: 30-35 minutes
Yields: 1 loaf

Ingredients:
1 cup warm water
2⅔ cup Knight's Nutritious GF Flour Blend
1 Tbsp. organic rice milk, unsweetened, lukewarm
½ Tbsp. organic clover honey
¾ tsp. organic xanthan gum
1½ tsp. organic sea salt
2 Tbsp. dairy and soy-free cheese, finely chopped
1-1½ Tbsp. organic Italian seasoning
2 Tbsp. diary and soy-free butter, melted
1½ tsp. organic active dry yeast
2 cage-free organic eggs

Instructions:
Preheat oven to 350 degrees.

Warm the honey and butter until both are melted; stir and set aside.
Combine the flour, salt, xanthan gum, Italian seasoning, and yeast in
the bowl of a stand mixer. Slowly beat the warm water and rice milk
into the flour mixture until it forms small, crumbly balls. Beat in the
butter and honey mixture until completely blended. Finally, add in
the eggs one at a time while continuing to beat the mixture on a low
speed. When all the ingredients have been added, beat the dough on
high for 2-3 minutes to add air to it. The dough will be soft and very
sticky. Cover the dough and set in a warm place. Allow it to rise for
1-2 hours or until it has doubled in size. Transfer the dough to a well-
buttered cast iron or glass bread pan and let it rise for another hour.
Lightly brush the surface of the dough with melted butter or water to
add more moisture to it. Cook for 25-30 minutes or until it is golden
brown. Cool on a cooling rack. Serve and enjoy!

MOM'S PANCAKES

Preparation time: 5 minutes
Cook time: 20 minutes
Yields: 10

Ingredients:
1 free-range organic egg
1 cup organic rice milk, unsweetened
1 Tbsp. extra virgin olive oil
1 cup Knight's Nutritious GF Flour Blend
½ tsp. organic sea salt
1 tsp. organic baking powder

Instructions:
In a small bowl, combine all the ingredients and stir well, removing the majority of the flour clumps. Preheat a cast iron griddle to medium heat. Coat with a light layer of dairy and soy-free butter. Cook first side of pancake until the surface is covered in tiny bubbles. Flip the pancake. Cook the second side for 1-2 minutes. Remove from heat and serve with butter, syrup, and fresh fruit.

Hint: For thinner pancakes, reduce the baking powder by half and the consistency will be more like a crepe.

MOM'S PANCAKES

SOFT AND SWEET HONEY BREAD

Preparation time: 30 minutes
Cook time: 25-30 minutes
Yields: 1 loaf

Ingredients:
3¼ cup Knight's Nutritious GF Flour Blend
2 tsp. organic active dry yeast
1 tsp. organic sea salt
1¼ tsp. organic xanthan gum
¾ cup organic rice milk, unsweetened, lukewarm
⅓ cup organic clover honey
¼ cup dairy and soy-free butter
3 cage-free organic eggs

Instructions:
Preheat oven to 350 degrees.
Warm the honey and butter until melted. Stir and set it aside. Combine the flour, salt, xanthan gum, and yeast in the bowl of a stand mixer. Slowly beat the warm rice milk into the flour mixture until it forms small, crumbly balls. Beat in the butter mixture. Next, add in the eggs one at a time while continuing to beat on low speed. When all ingredients have been added, beat on high for 2-3 minutes to add air to the dough. The dough will have a very sticky consistency. Cover it and set it in a warm place. Allow it to rise for 1-2 hours or until it doubles in size. Transfer the dough to a well-buttered and floured cast iron or glass bread pan and let it rise for another hour. When risen, lightly brush the surface of the dough with melted butter or water to add moisture to it. Cook for 25-30 minutes or until golden brown. Let it cool until the bread sweats in the pan. Remove it from the pan and continue to cool on a cooling rack. Serve with warm butter and enjoy!

SWEET MUFFINS

Preparation time: 15 minutes
Cook time: 20 minutes
Yields: 12

Ingredients:
1 cage-free organic egg
¾ cup organic coconut milk, unsweetened
½ cup extra virgin olive oil
2 cup Knight's Nutritious GF Flour Blend
⅓ cup agave nectar (more if needed)
3 tsp. organic baking powder
1 tsp. organic sea salt

Instructions:
Preheat oven to 400 degrees.
In the bowl of a stand mixer, combine the flour, baking powder, and salt. Add in the egg, coconut milk, oil, and agave nectar. Blend until smooth.

Butter and lightly flour a 12 cup cast iron muffin pan. Place a heaping scoop of batter in each cup. Bake for 20 minutes or until the tops of muffins are lightly browned.

*Variation 1: For Cinnamon-Apple Muffins: Add ½ cup of diced organic apples, rolled heavily in cinnamon. Increase the agave nectar by one tsp. and sprinkle cinnamon over each muffin before cooking.

*Variation 2: For Blueberry Muffins: Add ½ cup of fresh organic blueberries. Increase the agave nectar by 1 tsp.

TENDER TORTILLAS

Preparation time: 20 minutes
Cook time: 40 minutes
Yields: 12

Ingredients:
3 cups Knight's Nutritious GF Flour Blend
1 tsp. organic sea salt
½ tsp. organic baking powder
⅓ cup extra virgin olive oil
1 cup warm water

Instructions:
In the bowl of a stand mixer, combine the flour, baking powder, and sea salt and mix until well combined. Add in the oil and water. Beat for 1 minute at medium speed or until the dough begins to form small balls. Reduce the speed and beat on low until dough becomes smooth. Move the dough to a well-floured pastry mat and separate it into 12 equal sized balls. Flour a rolling pin and lightly flour the top of each ball of dough. Carefully roll out each ball until slightly see-through (about the size of a regular tortilla.) Keep the mat and rolling pin well-floured throughout process. Keep the uncooked tortillas separated with parchment to prevent sticking while waiting to be cooked. (The dough will dry out very rapidly so roll the tortillas out quickly and cook immediately.)
Bring a cast iron skillet up to medium heat. Carefully transfer one uncooked tortilla to the skillet and cook for 30 seconds on each side. Remove from heat and cool. Repeat until all tortillas are cooked. Serve and enjoy!

Hint: To freeze: Place parchment paper between each tortilla and store in a Ziploc bag to preserve freshness.

TURKEY STUFFING

Preparation time: 1 hour
Cook time: 30 minutes
Serves: 5

Ingredients:
Stuffing Bread:
1 cup organic rice milk, unsweetened, lukewarm
1½ Tbsp. organic active dry yeast
3 cage-free organic eggs
⅛ cup organic clover honey
2½ cup Knight's Nutritious GF Flour Blend
1 tsp. organic xanthan gum
1 tsp. organic baking powder
1 tsp. organic sea salt

Stuffing Sauce:
2-3 tsp. extra virgin olive oil
2 tsp. organic minced garlic
1 cup fresh organic onion, chopped
1 cup organic carrot, shredded
1 cup organic celery, chopped
2 tsp. organic Italian seasoning
2 tsp. organic poultry seasoning
½ tsp. organic sage
½ tsp. organic thyme
½ tsp. organic oregano
½ tsp. organic basil
½ tsp. organic rosemary
1 cage-free organic egg, slightly beaten
1½-3 cups organic chicken stock (3 cups will make very soupy stuffing)

Instructions:
Stuffing Bread:

Preheat oven to 350 degrees.

Warm honey until melted. Stir and set aside. In the bowl of a stand mixer, combine the flour, salt, xanthan gum, powder, and yeast. Slowly beat the warm milk into the flour mixture until if forms small, crumbly balls. Add in the honey and mix until completely blended. Toss in the eggs one at a time, while continuing to beat on low. When all the ingredients have been added, beat the dough on high for 2-3 minutes to add air to it. The dough will be very sticky. Cover it and put in a warm place. Allow the dough to rise for 1-2 hours or until it doubles in size. Once it has risen, move the dough to a well-buttered and floured cast iron or glass bread pan and let it rise for another hour. Lightly brush the batter with melted butter or water to add moisture to the dough. Cook for 25-30 minutes or until the top is golden brown. Cool on a cooling rack and cut or tear it into bite size pieces. Leave the pieces uncovered for a day, or bake at 200 degrees until dry.

Stuffing Sauce:

In a large skillet over low heat, sauté the garlic, onions, carrots, and celery in olive oil. Add in the seasonings and stir well. Pour in enough chicken stock to ensure that bread will be moist, but not soupy. Remove from heat and stir in the egg and mix to combine. Finally, pour the warm sauce over the bread crumbs. Thoroughly coat all the crumbs with sauce. Transfer the stuffing to a well-greased 9x13 pan. Bake for 30 minutes or until top is lightly toasted. Serve and enjoy!

WAFFLES

Preparation time: 10 minutes
Cook time: 5-6 minutes
Yields: 12

Ingredients:
2 cage-free organic eggs
1¾ cup organic rice milk, unsweetened
½ cup extra virgin olive oil
2 cups Knight's Nutritious GF Flour Blend
3 tsp. organic baking soda
1 Tbsp. organic clover honey

Instructions:
In a medium sized bowl, combine the flour and baking soda. Add in the milk, honey, oil, and eggs. Whisk until smooth. Preheat a griddle to medium heat. Pour 1 cup of batter onto the griddle. Cook for 5-6 minutes or until golden brown. Serve with dairy and soy-free butter, maple syrup, and fresh organic fruit.

MEET THE AUTHOR

Leah Knight is a freelance writer, skilled recipe creator, classically trained professional singer and private music teacher. When faced with challenging health issues, Leah and her husband Jason began to follow a strict dietary regimen. Dedication to this way of life has resulted in a more balanced emotional and stable physical existence for both Leah and Jason. Using her new found energy, Leah has created a variety of delicious alternative recipes, expanding a focused diet into a well-rounded and interesting plan. Leah and Jason reside in Fargo, North Dakota.

CPSIA information can be obtained at www.ICGtesting.com
Printed in the USA
LVOW10*1235100515

437853LV00002B/3/P

9 781496 944931